PROTECTION AMID CHAOS

COLUMBIA STUDIES IN MIDDLE EAST POLITICS

COLUMBIA STUDIES IN MIDDLE EAST POLITICS

MARC LYNCH, SERIES EDITOR

Columbia Studies in Middle East Politics presents academically rigorous, well-written, relevant, and accessible books on the rapidly transforming politics of the Middle East for an interested academic and policy audience.

PROTECTION AMID CHAOS

THE CREATION OF PROPERTY RIGHTS IN PALESTINIAN REFUGEE CAMPS

NADYA HAJJ

Columbia University Press
New York

Columbia University Press
Publishers Since 1893
New York   Chichester, West Sussex
cup.columbia.edu

Library of Congress Cataloging-in-Publication Data
Names: Hajj, Nadya, author.
Title: Protection amid chaos : the creation of property rights in
   Palestinian refugee camps / Nadya Hajj.
Description: New York : Columbia University Press, 2017. |
   Series: Columbia studies in Middle East politics |
   Includes bibliographical references and index.
Identifiers: LCCN 2016015785 (print) | LCCN 2016020769 (ebook) |
   ISBN 9780231180627 (cloth : alk. paper) | ISBN 9780231542920 (electronic)
Subjects: LCSH: Refugee property, Palestinian—Lebanon. |
   Refugee property, Palestinian—Jordan. | Right of property—Lebanon. |
   Right of property—Jordan. | Refugee camps—Lebanon. |
   Refugee camps—Jordan. | Palestinian Arabs—Claims.
Classification: LCC KMK2695.P35 H35 2017 (print) | LCC KMK2695.P35 (ebook) |
   DDC 323.4/6091749274—dc23
LC record available at https://lccn.loc.gov/2016015785

Printed in the United States of America

c 10 9 8 7 6 5 4 3 2 1

Cover design: Lisa Hamm

for Baba, Mama, Patrick, and Leila

CONTENTS

FIGURES, MAPS, AND TABLE

FIGURES

MAPS

TABLE

ACKNOWLEDGMENTS

I began field research in the summer of 2004 and completed my last interview in June of 2012. Over the course of those eight years, many people made this project possible. Linda and Hatim Hajj, aka Mama and Baba, provided me with enormous support. Baba was my research aide and transcriber on many trips. His intimate knowledge of camp life and his technical background helped me orient my research. Mama sent encouraging emails and kept me going when things got tough. Patrick, my husband, anchored me during the endeavor and kept the home fires burning while I spent time away. Leila, my daughter, provided the best distraction from writing and the most potent motivation for finishing the project. Elaine and Ray encouraged me to finish writing even when it got hard. The entire Hajj family in Jordan, Lebanon, and Syria kept me fed, hydrated, laughing, and safe during my research. I am lucky to have so many cousins. Thank you.

Many colleagues helped improve the manuscript. At Emory University, Rick Doner, Thomas Remington, Carrie Wickham, and Tracy Yandle provided good ideas during the earliest inception of the research. The Political Science Department at Emory provided helpful research funding in 2004, 2005, and 2007. I am also thankful for the generous research support that Wellesley College offered me as a new faculty member. This support made it possible for me to complete the last iteration of interviews in 2012. In addition, the Northeast Middle East Political Science Working Group meetings in 2012, 2013, and 2014 were the best. I found my tribe of scholars that shared my passion for everything to do with the Middle East and political science. The whole crew of senior and junior scholars provided critical and helpful feedback that made a real difference in how I thought about my research. The careful reviews I received from Melani Cammett, Amaney Jamal, Marc Lynch, Jeannie Sowers, and many others at the Project on Middle East Political Science Junior Scholars Conference in 2014 propelled this research to a much better place. The *Journal of Comparative Politics* generously permitted me to reprint a portion of a previously published article: "Institutional Formation in Transitional Settings." The anonymous reviewers and my editor, Anne Routon, helped polish the manuscript and make it a book. Thank you.

Finally, I am thankful to the hundreds of Palestinians that shared their stories with me. I am honored. You deserve a voice and I hope I did it justice. Of course, those who helped me shoulder no blame for any errors, omissions, interpretations, or conclusions in this book. I take responsibility for those.

Nadya Hajj

ABBREVIATIONS
AND TRANSLATIONS

CC	Camp Committee, Lebanon
CSIC	Camp Services Improvement Committee, Jordan
DFLP	Democratic Front for the Liberation of Palestine
DPA	Department of Palestinian Affairs, Jordan
GAPAR	General Administration for Palestine Arab Refugees, Syria
GUPS	General Union of Palestinian Students
GUPW	General Union of Palestine Workers
NBC	Nahr al-Bared Camp
NIE	New Institutional Economics
PARI	Palestinian Arab Refugee Institute, Syria
PFLP	Popular Front for the Liberation of Palestine
PLO	Palestine Liberation Organization
UAR	United Arab Republic

UN	United Nations
UNCCP	United Nations Conciliation Commission for Palestine
UNHCR	United Nations High Commission on Refugees
UNRWA	United Nations Relief and Works Agency

NOTE ON ARABIC TRANSLITERATION

Throughout the book, I use a modified version of the *International Journal of Middle East Studies* transliteration system guidelines while retaining transliterations of Palestinian place names and figures.

PROTECTION AMID CHAOS

INTRODUCTION

Property rights are not supposed to exist in Palestinian refugee camps. At least the existing scholarly record does not predict their presence. After all, why would a marginalized community living in uncertain political economic conditions go to all the trouble and effort of crafting institutions that lay claim to assets in a refugee camp? Yet a routine interview with a Palestinian refugee led to the discovery of formal legal titles inside refugee camps strewn across Lebanon and Jordan. The discovery triggered a new understanding of the potential for institutional innovation and evolution in transitional political landscapes, places that lack a stable sovereign state with the legal jurisdiction to define and enforce institutions.

This routine interview with a Palestinian refugee was book-ended by an extraordinary political event. On September 2, 2007, the Lebanese government declared that Nahr al-Bared Palestinian refugee camp (NBC) was completely destroyed. The destruction was caused by a conflict between the Lebanese government and Fatah al-Islam, a clandestine militia group. Initially, it was unclear if the camp would be rebuilt. However, on June 23, 2008, donors, Lebanese government officials, the Palestine Liberation Organization (PLO), and United Nations Relief Works Agency (UNRWA) representatives voted unanimously to rebuild NBC and developed a "Master Plan" for reconstruction (I-92L).[1] Reconstruction officially began on April 1, 2010. The new camp would better attend to health and sanitation considerations, provide better infrastructure, accommodate all previous residences and businesses, and maintain the traditional social fabric of the old camp (I-90L, I-92L). After years of research in the old NBC, I re-interviewed the respondents post-conflict.

In interviews with Palestinians from Nahr al-Bared, refugees that had lived in the old camp since its inception in 1951 maintained serious misgivings about living in the new NBC. One man explained,

> Of course, I want to return to NBC. But it will be very different there and most of all I will feel dispossessed for a second time. Do you know why? It is because I hear that I won't own my new place there, like I did before! I used to own a home in the camp that I was proud of—we worked for sixty years to scrape together a life. Now, we can't own, rent, or sell parts of our new home. (I-70L)

What did he mean he *owned* his home *in the refugee camp*? When asked what he meant by "ownership" of his former home, the refugee produced a tattered property title that looked like the one shown in appendix A. It was a formal legal property title establishing the owner's right to use, sell, protect, and benefit from the ownership of his home. After probing further, he said there were repositories of file cabinets stuffed with property titles lining the walls of camp committee (CC) offices in refugee camps throughout Lebanon.

The camp committee office might have looked like a boring meeting room to an unwitting observer, but it was, in fact, filled with proof that legal titles establishing ownership of the right to use, sell, and protect an investment or asset had developed in the most unlikely of political spaces. The file clerk at the CC permitted closer inspection of the titles. His cigarette was burning down to a nub and the hazy smoke filling the room only added to the moment, pregnant with drama.

Like Indiana Jones tearing through cobwebs and finding the Holy Grail, I squeaked open a metal file cabinet drawer and discovered hard-copy evidence of property titles in refugee camps all over Lebanon and Jordan. It was as if an unknown historical treasure had been unearthed. The NBC title dated back to 2004 and the Beddawi title was a blank copy from 2012, but both are generally reflective of the property title template used in camps across Lebanon and Jordan since 1969. Subsequent research trips to Palestinian refugee camps in Jordan confirmed the presence of formal titles housed in camp services improvement committees (CSIC) too. A certified Arabic-English translator translated the documents for easy understanding.

The NBC document reveals that one seller and two buyers (brothers) transferred a title to an apartment in the camp. The stamp in the bottom right corner identifies that the CC witnessed the contract and collected payment for the service. The blank title from Beddawi camp echoes the findings in NBC. The new owner of the apartment was given the sole right to reap the benefits of the property and to sell or trade it if desired. The text of this title transfer reveals that refugees clearly delineated property in the camps by specifying the location and the size of the space that was owned. In addition, title transfers reveal that property was in fact alienable, meaning that resources could be bought or sold inside the camps. While transitional landscapes like refugee camps are challenging places where war and destruction may happen, they are also places where political imagination and economic opportunity may develop. As a result, transitional landscapes need to be theoretically recast as much more than places of hopelessness and despair.

The evidence of property rights in Palestinian refugee camps across the Middle East encouraged a central research question: How and why did property rights develop in transitional settings? Using the data from hundreds of interviews, I traced the evolution of property rights from informal understandings of ownership to formal legal institutions that define and enforce claims to assets and resources inside the camps. The Palestinian refugees' central narrative is that they tried to create order out of chaos in a transitional space. Property rights, both informal and formal, were one tool that Palestinians used to protect their assets and their community from outside domination and state incorporation.

After their arrival in the camps, Palestinians devised their own systems of protection through property rights by strategically drawing upon shared experiences from life before the camps. In the absence of a state, refugees deployed bits and pieces of their pre-1948 life like village codes of honor and shame that could easily work in the challenging realities of camp life. These malleable informal practices protected assets and insulated community affairs from outsiders that sought to dominate and control the camps. Over time, as the camps became more economically complex and new outside political groups wrestled to control the community, refugees struggled to craft property rights that protected their community assets while buffering them from outsider predation. In these conditions, refugees melded parts of their own informal property practices with those of more powerful outsiders. This strategy protected assets and permitted them to find some autonomy from state incorporation. The formal property rights Palestinian refugees built in concert with outsiders were imperfect institutions, but they are testament to the resilience of a community navigating the precarious politics of a transitional landscape and finding some measure of protection.

ORGANIZATION OF THE BOOK

This book maps how Palestinians found protection through property rights in refugee camps. In chapter 1, I develop the central argument, define key terms, specify cases, and describe data sources. In chapter 2, I trace the formation of informal property rights in camps across Lebanon and Jordan. In the early years, Palestinians confronted a significant degree of communal tension when they were thrust into unfamiliar refugee camps. In Lebanon and Jordan, an informal system of property rights evolved organically. This pattern of property rights formation was consistent with a spontaneous order approach because it was based on easily replicable pre-1948 experiences in property ownership. Following the 1967 Arab-Israeli War, the Cairo Accords in 1969, and Black September in 1970, the camps in Jordan and Lebanon took divergent pathways to protection through property rights.

In chapter 3, I examine how Palestinians brokered agreements with the Jordanian government to create a formal system of rules. Jordanians hoped to control and co-opt the refugee camps after Black September. Though Palestinians enjoyed limited citizenship benefits in Jordan, they still resisted incorporation and pushed for protection through informal Palestinian practices of title adjudication and enforcement. A compromise was reached whereby Palestinian and Jordanian titling and enforcement practices were melded to protect assets from predation and to resist total state incorporation. In working with outsiders, refugees gave up a significant portion of Palestinian political freedom by submitting to the will of Jordanians in some areas of property enforcement.

In chapter 4, I discuss the Palestinians' negotiations of property rights with Fatah, a revolutionary Palestinian political organization founded by Yasser Arafat and other key Palestinian leaders, in camps across Lebanon. Fatah's arrival in 1969 created a new ruling coalition inside the camps that forced Palestinian refugees to renegotiate the system of property rights. Fatah pushed for the formalization of titles whereas the community hoped to preserve their existing informal system of protection. Despite Fatah's revolutionary appeal, Palestinian refugees hoped to protect assets from predation and Fatah dominance. They injected the formal system of property rights with informal community practices in adjudication. Even though the community managed to insulate itself from parts of Fatah's dominance, the new system of formal property rights gave Fatah inordinate control in the realm of enforcement. In the case of shared resources like water and electricity, Fatah often plundered the system for political purposes. The friction between protection of assets and submission to Fatah's power was an unresolved tension in the transitional landscape. Moreover, the tension highlights the limits of locally contrived property rights.

In chapter 5, I further test the limits of locally developed institutions. Palestinian refugees in Northern Lebanon brokered a new system of property rules with the Lebanese military following the destruction and reconstruction of NBC in 2007. Again the resilience of Palestinian refugees in finding protection after another dispossession from their property is underscored. But the new system of protection came at the price of Lebanese military domination and enforcement. The book concludes with a summary of major findings and the exportability of lessons to other communities living in transitional landscapes around the world.

1

A THEORY OF PROPERTY RIGHTS FORMATION IN PALESTINIAN REFUGEE CAMPS

In 1948, we left my village in Palestine. I was a young child, maybe eight years old. But I remember how hard it was. We lost our home, our farm, and our grazing lands. . . . We were terrified. We left with anything we could carry on our backs, even our mattresses! We walked all the way to the southern border of Lebanon. Can you imagine? Families with old people and young children walking such a long distance. After arriving in the south [of Lebanon] we thought that we would return to our home in a couple of months, at most. No one had any idea our situation would last so long. My mother sold almost all her mahr (dowry) to keep us alive but we still ran out of money. Our savings depleted. The Lebanese didn't want thousands of us crowding the border indefinitely. So with the help of the Red Cross and UNRWA they put us up in old French-built military barracks before loading us onto big trucks or rail cars to take us to the north of Lebanon. The Red Cross had created a census in 1949 that they shared with UNRWA. We were assigned a registration number that corresponded to our family name. They gave each family of six to ten people a tent to share, a stove, and rations, and then we were sent to Nahr al-Bared camp. The rest of our village was put there too. But other villages from the same region in Palestine were also there. In the first two years of the camps there were lots of fights between villages over everything from land to tents. It was fawdah (chaos). But after a while we settled in. There was no choice but to make rules to protect us. Now, these rules weren't written down. But we all understood who owned what. It was shameful for your family if you were caught stealing from another family. Family honor and our faith in Allah and the Quran helped us create order. We protected ourselves in a hard place.

—INTERVIEW TRANSCRIPT OF ALI L., CAMP HISTORIAN,
MAY 24, 2012, IN TRIPOLI, LEBANON

The subject matter of creation is chaos.

—BARNETT NEWMAN, ABSTRACT PAINTER

Ali L.'s story of his journey from Palestine to a refugee camp in Northern Lebanon provides a glimpse into how Palestinians found protection in chaos. He describes how Palestinians navigated life after the *Nakbah* or Catastrophe of 1948 following the war between the Arabs and the Israelis. He sheds light on the creation of property rights, a bundle of rules that govern the ownership of assets, created to protect the community. His story represents a departure from the usual story about Palestinian refugees.

Our understanding of Palestinian refugees is usually gleaned from reports of the camps as hopeless places filled with helpless people. Certainly, Palestinians have faced seemingly insurmountable obstacles in Jordan and Lebanon. Many Palestinians arrived in the camps in 1948 with only the clothes on their backs. They lived for close to twenty years without clean running water and electricity. They are inured to war and political instability. However, an appraisal of Palestinian refugee camps as places bereft of innovation and entrepreneurial spirit only presents a partial portrait of life in the camps. The Palestinian refugees' central narrative is that they tried to find protection in chaos. Palestinians built property rights, both informal and formal, to protect the community from the daily chaos of camp life. How did Palestinians manage institutional innovation and evolution in such challenging conditions?

In brief, this book endeavors to show the complicated story of how normal people placed in extraordinarily difficult conditions managed to create protections for their assets and community through property rights. The research focuses on Palestinians living in seven refugee camps in Lebanon and Jordan. Using interview transcripts with two hundred Palestinian refugees, legal title documents, memoirs, and United Nations Relief Works Agency (UNRWA) archives, I traced the evolution of property rights from informal understandings of ownership to formal legal claims of assets to shed light on how communities thrive in challenging political economic spaces. Initially, Palestinians deployed bits and pieces of their pre-refugee life to craft informal property claims that met the challenges of living in refugee camps. Later, as the camps increased in complexity with expanding markets and new outsiders entering the political fray, Palestinians strategically melded their informal practices with the formal rules of political outsiders. Within the constraints of refugee life, Palestinians, to varying degrees of success, managed to protect their assets and community from outsider predation.

KEY CONCEPTS

Before an elaboration of the central thesis, I clarify key concepts embedded in the study of how Palestinians established protection through property rights in refugee camps. Specifically, I define property rights and explain how property rights might offer protection in transitional contexts. These definitions serve as the foundation for unpacking the notion of a transitional political space and for understanding why a Palestinian refugee camp can be considered such a place.

PROPERTY RIGHTS

Property rights are a bundle of agreements that establish the right to use, sell, and protect an investment or asset. Successful property rights meet two conditions: they define ownership and they are enforceable.

Ostrom et al. note that successful property rights are able to "fully define ownership and effectively sanction violators" (1994, 267).

In an informal sense, a community would respect the boundaries of one person's asset, even if the lines were invisible and not written down. Moreover, communities would have shared norms of punishing individuals that trampled on the assets of others. In a formal sense, property rights define ownership with a legal title and enforce claims with a judicial system that metes out and upholds punishments. Both formal and informal property rights are important for a community's ability to protect itself from predation.

Formal property rights are not necessarily better or stronger than informal ones. What matters most is the community's ability to define and enforce assets, regardless of whether they are based on shared norms or are legally codified. They are not a one-size-fits-all institutional arrangement. They work best when they are adapted to the local political economic landscape. For example, Qian (2003) compares institutional formation in China to post-Communist Russia. He asserts that China was more successful than post-Communist Russia in creating property rights because of the ability of Chinese firms and local officials to search for "feasible" institutions of protection in the face of imperfect market conditions. The transitional institutions in China worked because they simultaneously achieved two objectives. First, they improved economic efficiency. Second, the institutions were compatible with the interests of those in power (Qian 2003). Though they were not perfect in the sense of being fully codified and enforced based on an established judicial system, they were feasible given local conditions. From this perspective, both informal and formal property rights play an important role in offering communities protection.

Beyond this basic definition and measurement scheme, property rights are powerful indicators of a community's social, economic, and political health (Rodrik 2003). If they are present, they usually indicate that a large segment of society experiences protection against expropriation and predation from private agents. In addition, they signal a measure of stability and effective constraints on the arbitrary and extractive behavior of political elites. The key point is that property rights offer protection to communities. In particular, property rights give individuals the ability to protect financial assets or investments from predation.

TRANSITIONAL SPACES

Communities living in transitional landscapes could greatly benefit from the protection that property rights might offer because these spaces represent the razor's edge between control and political wilderness (Curzon 1907). Political geographers optimistically believed that by the twentieth century most transitional spaces had disappeared and been replaced by boundaries that were hard and fast lines (Prescott 1987, 1). According to scholars, states extended their authority over much of the world, and "primary settlements" or places where the state was taking possession of a territory for the first time were mostly consolidated by the twentieth century. The expansion of the American government over Western territories and the end of the "wild, wild West" was the classically touted example of state consolidation over a transitional settlement. Though lawlessness and violence were once pervasive on the Western frontier, American central governance slowly quieted the violence and brought the territories under the rule of law (Anderson and Hill 2004; Knight 1992; Libecap 1989). Amazonian communities in Brazil were also consolidated in a similar manner through integration into central governance structures (Alston, Libecap, and Mueller 1999). According to researchers, this consolidation was often driven by economic desires for state control over valuable natural resources like mines and water. Scholars optimistically predicted an end to transitional spaces. In particular, it was not problematized that consolidation efforts could ever break down or that sovereignty could devolve into political wilderness.

Though political geographers expected an end to transitional spaces, pockets cropped up in weakly consolidated states during the latter half of the twentieth century following the end of World War II. These areas mark zones that separate settled and lawless regions of the state. In most cases, these transitional spaces are less the result of physical isolation and more reflective of the weak will and/or capacity of states to assert their dominance. Pockets of these spaces abound in post-Communist transitional states like the Ukraine, peripheral provinces in western China, and failing states rife with civil conflict throughout the Middle East and Africa. Notably, the distinguishing feature in these political landscapes is that the state is present and has legal authority to control a territory, but is not able or willing to extend its authority.

My central focus is on a less-studied but still critical type of transitional space. The Palestinian case is an example of a transitional landscape because it represents a contested space based on some legal prevention that creates purposeful pockets of anarchy. In 1951, Arab states wanted to absolve themselves of the burden of caring for Palestinian refugees, so they voted to exclude Palestinian refugees from the 1951 United Nations High Commission on Refugees (UNHCR) Convention ("1951 Convention") that established the protections and rights of refugees around the world. Though the UNRWA furnishes Palestinian refugee camps with basic human rights services like education, health services, and food and water rations, the camps are institutional landscapes *intentionally* void of a state with the legal will and capacity to define and enforce institutions. Refugee camps, like the Palestinian ones in Lebanon and Jordan, occupy this space because they are politically ambiguous spaces by design. In this political vacuum, a variety of stakeholders ranging from humanitarian aid groups to nascent states and nonstate political groups fight for power and authority over the community. In response to the ambiguity, the community devises its own system of protection to contend with outsiders.

THE PALESTINIAN TRANSITIONAL SPACE

To fully appreciate the Palestinian case as a transitional space, a brief historical review assesses the origins of the Palestinian refugee situation. Though some consider the Palestinian experience to be unique, I push away from exceptionalist frameworks. Instead, I place Palestinian refugee camps in comparative context with other communities living in transitional conditions. The United Nations recently reported an astounding number of refugees, more than any time since World War II. The Palestinian case provides an excellent template for others communities hoping to find protection in transitional spaces.

In November 1947, a UN resolution created the state of Israel, a small territory roughly the size of Massachusetts that was inhabited for 1,200 years by an Arab majority.[1] On May 14, 1948, Israel proclaimed its independence. Palestinians refer to this historic moment as *Nakbah* or the Catastrophe. The partition and subsequent war over territory between Israelis and Palestinians during 1948 and 1949 set in motion a messy political and military conflict that remains unresolved today. Contested historical accounts provide different understandings of 1948. Israelis, Palestinians, British officials, American leaders, "New Historians," and policy makers offer conflicting perspectives.[2] Resolving the historical debate over 1948 lies outside the scope of this book; however, it is clear that 1948 marks the genesis of the Palestinian refugee crisis and the birth of Palestinian refugee camps as transitional places. It was a humanitarian catastrophe and the first refugee crisis confronting the newly formed United Nations following World War II. The birth of the Palestinian refugee "problem" in 1948 left most Palestinians with few assets and little more than the clothes on their backs (Schiff 1995).

During 1948 and 1949, Arab governments primarily bore the responsibility for refugee relief. In August 1949, the United Nation's Clapp Mission assessed the repercussions of and the potential solutions for the 1948–1949 war between the Israelis and the Arabs.

In total, the mission estimated 726,000 refugees, of whom 652,000 were classified as "in need" (Brand 1988, 150). The magnitude and size of the refugee crisis prompted the Clapp Mission to recommend the formation of an organization to specifically handle the Palestinian refugee crisis (Brand 1988, 150). On December 8, 1949, UN Resolution 302 created the United Nations Relief and Works Agency for Palestinian refugees in the Near East (UNRWA) (Brand 1988, 150). It officially began operations on May 1, 1950 (Brand 1988, 150).

There was no provision in UNRWA's mandate for determining who qualified as a Palestinian refugee and therefore was eligible for assistance (Takkenberg 1998, 69). UNRWA's provisional definition of eligible persons developed while relief work was conducted on the ground inside the camps. Several revisions to the definition occurred over the years. To qualify as a Palestinian refugee under UNRWA's mandate, "a person must have lost his home and livelihood and reside in a country where UNRWA operates" (Takkenberg 1998, 68). In addition, UNRWA provisionally extends refugee status to descendants of these refugees, though there is still, even today, "no valid legal definition of a 'Palestinian refugee' beyond the provisional definition of UNRWA" (Takkenberg 1998, 68).

On December 3, 1949, just a short time before the creation of UNRWA, the UN general assembly adopted Resolution 319, which established the United Nations High Commissioner for Refugees (UNHCR). These statutes were adopted a year later at the first international refugee convention, "Convention Relating to the Status of Refugees of 28 July 1951" (known as the "1951 Convention") (Knudsen 2009, 53). The 1951 Convention established a universal definition of refugee status and prohibits the forcible return of refugees. It applies the universal definition to all refugees after January 1, 1951, but Palestinian refugees from 1948 were excluded from the policy. Arab states feared that applying the 1951 definition to Palestinians would make the Arab states "responsible for their upkeep" (Knudsen 2009, 53). Arab states proposed an amendment to the 1951 draft that explicitly excluded Palestinian refugees that were already supported by UNRWA. In this context, a purposeful pocket of legal ambiguity or "protection gap" exists for Palestinians. As a result, they occupy a transitional space where no international or regional stakeholder can lay legal claim to the protection of or legal sovereignty over Palestinian refugees (Knudsen 2009, 54). In these conditions, Palestinians devised their own institutions for protection, and property rights were one strategy among many they used.

THEORIES ON PROPERTY RIGHTS FORMATION

The existing scholarly record does not predict the formation of property rights, either informal or formal, in the transitional context of Palestinian refugee camps. The real challenge of institutional formation is not so much knowing where to end up but learning how stakeholders search for a *feasible path* in a particular setting and move toward the goal.[3] Institutions, like property rights, are dynamic and reflect the strategic interaction of negotiating communities with their contextual setting (North and Weingast 1989). Every institution is realized on the ground through many stakeholders, power distributions, and incentives.[4] In searching for the feasible path, how do stakeholders construct informal or formal property rights in transitional settings?

There are two distinct causal pathways in the institutional origins literature. The spontaneous origins argument maintains that informal rules of property evolve spontaneously or without any process of collective choice. In particular, rules regarding ownership of property can evolve without conscious human design and can maintain themselves without *any* formal machinery, like a state, to enforce them (Sugden 1989). Scholars often point to the development of rules regarding ownership of driftwood collected on beaches or the use of a one-lane bridge when there are two cars waiting for safe passage. In these cases, communities do not convene a meeting and invite a state authority to determine a rule for how much driftwood a person can collect or which car can traverse the bridge first. Instead, in many cases, communities spontaneously develop rules of ownership.

Many of these spontaneous rules regarding ownership derive from shared social norms. There is debate within the spontaneous origins literature over the source of norms (Elster 1989). Some contend that norms develop out of sincere belief in what one should or ought to do and others maintain that they emerge from unconscious self-interest in how a community should govern ownership of an asset. These norms or shared understandings successfully generate rules, such as property rights, because they are easy to replicate (Elster 1989). Regardless of the source, the development of a stable pool of shared norms is key in explaining the spontaneous evolution of property rights when there is no authority like a state present (Axelrod 1984). Consistent with this view is the expectation that if market forces confer increasing value on an asset, then property rights will develop organically and maintain themselves without state intervention. In the context of Palestinian refugee camps, Sugden (1989) would not likely expect the spontaneous generation of informal property rights because there was not a stable pool of shared norms when new communities of refugees were thrust together for the first time in chaotic conditions.

In contrast, New Institutionalists maintain that there are myriad agents that might desire formal property rights when there is economic demand, but that third-party mechanisms for enforcement, in the form of state structures, are necessary to formalize institutions.[5] For example, New Institutionalists believe that in an increasingly diverse and competitive political economic landscape, shared norms of behavior are not enough. Institutions, like property rights, must develop to protect investments and facilitate trade. However, if a stakeholder has the authority to craft formalized property rights, then they are usually powerful enough and capable of abrogating those same rights (Haber et al 2002). Accordingly, the main stumbling block for the formation of formal property rights has been the creation of mechanisms that display the credible commitment of authorities to enforce and secure property rights claims (North 1995). To solve this enforcement dilemma, New Institutionalists hypothesize that state structures must act as third-party enforcers and create sanctions and incentives to protect property through a system of checks and balances.

The success of the Western European experience (for example, England) in crafting property rights and stimulating economic growth is the result of a representative government that shackles itself through a system of checks and balances to credibly protect individual claims to property rights from the arbitrary behavior of government (North 1995). In particular, economic historians often point to the triumph of England's Parliament in 1689 in crafting a set of impositions that held the government responsible for protecting property rights claims from arbitrary government behavior (North and Thomas 1973). Though most New Institutionalists tend to think that representative states are best suited to facilitate credible commitments, there is still some debate over the best type of state structure. However, most scholars tend to operate with the implicit assumption that some type of state with sovereign territorial integrity, internationally recognized borders, and the capacity to engage in contracts with other states is crucial for the formalization of property rights. In contrast, nonstate actors tend to lack territorial integrity, international recognition, and the capacity to engage in contracts with other states; these features hinder nonstates' ability to make credible commitments for the enforcement of property rights. In the absence of legal state authority in Palestinian refugee camps, scholars would not predict the formation of formal property rights.

Many studies in transitional settings currently theorize the intersection of informal demands for property rights and the timing and sequence of state intervention in completing the formalization process. De Soto outlines the process of property rights formalization for Peru's marginalized "informals." De Soto finds a pathway that begins with the arrival of rural migrants in Peru's urban areas; upon discovering inadequate resources and space for their economic aspirations, Peru's informals invade private or publicly held land, create an informal invasion contract among community stakeholders, establish an "expectative property right," and with increasing recognition by formal state legal systems, gradually establish formal property rights that are titled and sanctioned by the state (De Soto 1989, 23–25). Though the process is fraught with uncertainty and challenges, informals find their alternative options of landlessness, return to rural homes, and the potential opportunity of formal legal title worth the inherent risk of temporary informality.

This process is underpinned by an assumption among the informals of Peru that the Peruvian state will eventually incorporate their "expectative property right." Recent studies in China's periphery (Tsai 2002) also echo the ways in which local provincial models of institutional formation can inform state-level practices (Qian 2003). Shleifer shares this local to state connection perspective in tackling variation in economic growth in post-Communist countries (Shleifer 1997, 2001). Frye (2000) expands the study of institutional formalization by assessing points where local conditions intersect with state-level policy. He studies the interaction between state taxation policies on the formation of local private institutions that minimize cheating and increase security of property rights, thereby increasing social order in post-Communist Russia. More recently, Markus's (2012) study of Russia and Ukraine discovers that in the absence of state activism, alliances with stakeholders ranging from foreign investors, firms, and the community can enforce property rights with growth-enhancing effects. However, all of these studies are predicated on the notion that local communities will push for the state to formalize property rights.

Yet none of these causal arguments solve the puzzle of how Palestinian refugees crafted informal property rights that later evolved into formal systems in transitional spaces. The Palestinian refugee pathway to property rights formation and evolution belies existing models because there was no stable pool of shared norms, nor was there a sovereign state with the legal authority to create institutions present in the camps (Abouzeid 2003; Rubenberg 1983). Moreover, Palestinians were not "expectative" in creating rules. In fact, they actively resisted state incorporation.

Existing scholarship does not adequately attend to communities that actively resist incorporation into the state through formalization. In the case of many transitional communities, stateless people are sometimes forced to formalize against their will. Though the state or statelike political group credibly enforces property rights, the transitional community might resist incorporation into the state in order to protect their community and assets from more powerful neighbors and outside domination. Graeber finds that communities in anarchic conditions "begin creating the institutions of a new society 'within the shell of the old,' to expose, subvert, and undermine structures of domination" (2004, 7). Given the gaps in the current studies of institutional formation for transitional communities, I hypothesize another mode of institutional formation and evolution in transitional settings that builds on Graeber's (2004) assertion.

CENTRAL THESIS

In a transitional space, communities will seek protection in the face of chaos. Property rights, both informal and formal, offer one pathway of keeping community assets safe and, to varying degrees of success, resisting state incorporation in transitional settings. Communities in transitional settings build property rights that offer protection of assets and avoid state incorporation by (1) responding dynamically to shifts in political economic life and (2) strategically selecting bits and pieces of their "plastic" communal identity to meet those challenges.

First, communities in transitional spaces do not get "locked in" to one institutional design or pattern. Instead, institutional innovation is a dynamic and iterative process. At critical junctures in 1948, from 1969 to 1970, and in 2007, Palestinians responded dynamically to changes inside the refugee camps. They switched strategies for protection through property rights in response to shifting economic conditions and political alliances on the ground.

Thelen's study contributes to the story of Palestinian property rights formation because she rejects ideas that institutions are "locked in" once selected (2004, 31). She "elaborates an alternative perspective that underscores the contested nature of institutional development and in so doing, recovers the political dynamics, that drive institutional genesis and reproduction" (2004, 31). In her view, institutional formation and evolution are dynamic processes.

As Thelen (2004) points out, people can dynamically transform institutions through *layering*, or "grafting of new elements onto otherwise stable institutions," and *conversion*, or "the adoption of new goals or the incorporation of new group coalitions on which institutions are founded" (35–36). In keeping with her perspective, I find that as refugees confronted challenges to camp life, like an influx of wealth or the introduction of new political groups, Palestinians melded their ideas of ownership with new market realities and political coalitions. To avoid interaction with outsider judicial and penal systems in resolving property disputes, Palestinian refugee camps in Jordan and Lebanon built parallel systems of title enforcement that relied on the traditional community means of punishment and justice to protect assets at the local level. These parallel Palestinian systems worked even when outside groups ostensibly "enforced" formal property rights. A conversion strategy had an adaptive value that permitted Palestinians to preserve assets and resist complete state incorporation in the face of changing conditions.

Second, while there are myriad "traditional" ways a community could manage property and deal with new ruling coalitions, groups in transitional settings strategically convert certain parts of their group history to manage assets and insulate themselves from outsiders. Scott's (2009) study of "fractured" groups like the Zomias in *The Art of Not Being Governed* helps clarify how stateless people strategically dip into their well of institutional experience to protect themselves in challenging conditions. Whereas spontaneous order perspectives view norms or traditions as stable reservoirs of culture and practice, Scott maintains that the "traditions among stateless people are the 'jellyfish,' shape shifting, pliable form of custom, history, and law. They permit a certain 'drift' in content and emphasis over time—a strategic and interested re-adjustment" to confront the challenges they face (2009, 230). In transitional spaces, it is a "political calculation" to select bits and pieces of a group's history to enshrine in informal and formal institutions of property (2009, 43). Scott says, "In a world crowded with actors, most of whom like modern states, are more powerful than they [stateless communities], their freedom of invention is severely constricted" (2009, 244). Transitional communities crafted institutions in the best way they can, but not usually in circumstances of their choosing (2009, 244). To respond to these constraints, communities use parts of their identity for protection and to buffer against outsiders. He explains, "Like a chameleon's color adapting to the background, a vague shape shifting identity has great protective value and may, on that account, be actively cultivated by groups for whom a definite fixed identity might prove fatal . . . such plasticity affords outsiders no easy institutional access" (2009, 256).

Accordingly, Palestinian refugees strategically deployed community experiences of managing property to meet the demands of a changing political economic landscape that they were usually powerless to control. After the *Nakbah*, Palestinians responded to shocks by selectively drawing upon parts of their community history. They carefully drew upon traditional social units of organization like their *ahl* (family) or *hamula* (patrilineal clan) to collectively define ownership and notions of honor and *'ayb* (shame) to enforce claims.

For Palestinians, the ability to not get "locked in" and the strategic conversion of their group's identity had an adaptive value in threatening transitional conditions. In particular, "the more turbulent the social environment, the more frequently groups fission and recombine. . . . The Berbers are said to construct a genealogical warrant for virtually any alliance of convenience necessary to politics, grazing rights, or war" (Scott 2009, 233). Like the Berbers, the ability to convert parts of the group's institutional experiences to resist incorporation into new ruling coalitions was especially important when powerful groups not indigenous to the camps like the Jordanian state, Fatah, and the Lebanese military hoped to dominate and control the refugee camps.

Importantly, my subscription to the "jellyfish" nature of identity among Palestinians does not mean I believe Palestinians lacked an identity prior to the refugee camps. Some politicians, activists, and scholars seek to deny a uniquely Palestinian identity prior to 1948. They believe Palestinians prior to 1948 are a "myth."[6] Normally, these claims are used to justify the creation of Israel and to deny Palestinian calls for a "right to return." Contrary to this notion, I believe it is a peculiar and particular trait among stateless people, like the Zomias, the Berbers, and the Palestinians, to adopt purposefully ambiguous histories and traditions so that they can remain malleable and survive in conditions that threaten their survival.

Finally, in dealing with outsiders, Palestinians faced a tension in formalizing property rights. On one hand, property rights offered assets protection from predation. On the other hand, property rights negotiated with Jordan, Fatah, or the Lebanese military forced communal submission to outside enforcers. As Pierson observes, "Institution builders can never do just one thing" (2004, 115). In other words, forming property rights has intended and unintended consequences. As Thelen notes, "institutions designed to serve one set of interests often become 'carriers' of others as well" (2004, 33). For example, the German vocational training system ultimately served strong union interests, but the original framing legislation was mostly aimed at weakening unions (Thelen 2004). In the camps, the intention among refugees was to secure protection when negotiating with Lebanese, Fatah, and Jordanian authorities, though they unintentionally opened themselves up to predation by powerful outside enforcers too. Palestinians grappled with balancing order and communal freedom when building property rights. It is a tension that remains unresolved in the refugee camps.

RESEARCH DESIGN

I assessed how Palestinian refugees created protection through property rights in transitional settings by conducting interviews in seven refugee camps across Jordan and Lebanon. When I began my study in 2004, there was little preexisting data on how Palestinians created property rights at the micro level inside refugee camps in Jordan and Lebanon. During my initial research trip, I did a lot of what Fenno (1986) calls "soaking and poking" to see how Palestinians lived and ordered their daily lives in difficult conditions. I spoke in Arabic to anyone in the refugee camps who was willing to speak to me. I met with shopkeepers, religious officials, historians, lawyers, students, teachers, young mothers, old women, energetic young men, and religious elders. I was genuinely shocked to find residents showing me titles, like the one in appendix A, that evidenced formal property rights. The existing descriptive and theoretical literature on Palestinian camps never mentioned the presence of property rights. Moreover, I was surprised to learn about the rich history of how the community shifted strategies for protection over time. After my summer of research in 2004, I returned to graduate school and devoured the literature on institutional formation and Palestinian refugees. I endeavored to return to the Palestinian camps with a balanced strategy for selecting cases, an established set of interview questions, and strategies for limiting bias while getting the most complete story of how Palestinians created protection through property rights.

CASE SELECTION

After the initial research trip, seven cases were selected for further research. Three camps were selected in Jordan and four camps were selected in Lebanon. I used the UNRWA website to learn basic facts about the camps and selected camps that varied on conditions like the date of establishment, refugee background, and exposure to shocks.

For example, in Jordan, I evaluated three camps. Wihdat camp, also called "Amman New Camp," was one of four camps constructed to handle the early influx of 1948 refugees following *Nakbah*. In 1955, the camp was set up on 0.48 kilometers of land located southeast of the capital city of Amman. Initially, the camp accommodated 1,400 shelters. Today the camp houses 51,000 Palestinian refugees. Next, Baqa'a camp was one of six emergency camps set up following the 1967 Arab-Israeli War. It is one of the largest Palestinian refugee camps in Jordan and is located about 20 kilometers north of Amman. Originally, it housed 26,000 refugees, though that number has skyrocketed to 104,000 registered refugees today. Finally, Jerash camp, also known locally as "Gaza" camp, was established in 1968. It was created to house roughly 11,500 Palestinian refugees displaced from Gaza following the 1967 Arab-Israeli War. The camp covers an area of 0.75 kilometers and houses 24,000 refugees today.

Historical records show that Palestinian refugees have different legal statuses in Jordan based on their year of arrival and area of origin within Palestine. For example, in 1954, King Abdullah granted Palestinian refugees from the 1948 crisis Jordanian nationality and the benefits that go along with this status, such as access to courts, police protection, and the right to own property.[7] Notably, Palestinians did not officially "own" the land they lived on in the refugee camps, but they could own property outside the camps if they could afford it. This was a key difference between treatment in Jordan and Lebanon. Palestinians from the East Bank and West Bank that had 1948 "refugee status" were granted Jordanian nationality.[8]

Unlike Palestinians from 1948, Palestinians from Gaza who arrived in Jordan during the 1967 war were not issued Jordanian nationality because Gazans had previously been under Egyptian jurisdiction. Gazan Palestinians have in effect become refugees twice over. Most of the refugees now considered "Gazans" fled to the Gaza Strip for safety in 1948 and remained in refugee camps there until the 1967 war, when they were forced to flee to Jordan. With the

TABLE 1.1 CLASSIFICATIONS OF PALESTINIANS IN JORDAN BASED ON ORIGINS AND YEAR OF ARRIVAL. THIS CHART WAS ADAPTED FROM EL-ABED (2005).

ORIGIN/ YEAR OF ARRIVAL	RESIDENCE	PASSPORT TYPE	SERVICE ACCESSIBILITY
Jordanian-Palestinian 1948	Permanent in Jordan	Five-year passport with national ID number	Subject to 1954 law—can own property outside camps without ministerial approval
Palestinians of Gaza 1967	Permanent in Jordan	Temporary Two year passport	Not subject to 1954 law—need work permit, property ownership outside camps with approval of ministerial council

exception of a few families who had political connections and were able to obtain citizenship through royal decrees, most Gazans were treated as refugees with only partial benefits and sought shelter in one of the six emergency camps set up in the wake of the 1967 Arab-Israeli War. Gazan refugees hold temporary passports and must have a local Jordanian partner or receive the approval of a ministerial council to own property outside the refugee camps. Table 1.1 summarizes the political complexity of Palestinian refugee identity in Jordan based on their year of arrival and area of origin.[9]

The disparity in legal status between Palestinians from Gaza (since 1967) and non-Gazans (from 1948) would help me assess the strengths and pitfalls of formalizing property rights with outsiders like Jordan. A research design was constructed to see if Gazans faced greater vulnerability during formalization than 1948 Palestinians in Jordan. Research focused on three refugee camps that contained Palestinian populations with different legal statuses in Jordan. Wihdat refugee camp is primarily filled with residents that left Palestine in 1948 and therefore fall under the 1954 law. Baqa'a refugee camp is filled with a mixed population of refugees, with roughly 15 percent of refugees coming from the 1948 crisis and the rest from the 1967 crisis.[10] Jerash camp contained the highest concentration of Palestinian refugees that came from Gaza and held limited benefits in Jordan.

In Lebanon, I examined two camps in the north and two camps in the south. Beddawi and Nahr al-Bared (NBC) camps are located in Northern Lebanon near the port city of Tripoli, relatively close to the Syrian border. Beddawi was built in 1955 and is located about five kilometers from Tripoli on top of a hill. In Beddawi, shelters have indoor water supplies. The water system, sewerage, and storm water drainage systems were recently rehabilitated. Beddawi bore the brunt of the crisis at Nahr al-Bared, where fighting between the Lebanese armed forces and the radical militant group, Fatah Al-Islam, forced 27,000 refugees to flee. Beddawi's population swelled from 15,000 to 30,000 almost overnight. By mid-2009, around 10,000 displaced people were still living in Beddawi and surrounding areas. This put a huge strain on Beddawi's residents.

Nahr al-Bared was built in 1951 and is located roughly sixteen kilometers from Tripoli, directly on the Mediterranean Sea. Nahr al-Bared's population was estimated at 30,000 until 2007, when it was destroyed and roughly 27,000 people were forced to leave their homes. In the last eight years, UNRWA, international donors, and the Lebanese government have slowly rebuilt the camp. The reconstruction project involves 4,876 residential units, 1,105 shops, the UNRWA compound, and the camp's entire infrastructure.

In Southern Lebanon, I visited El-Buss and Rashidieh camps, located close to the border with Israel. El-Buss refugee camp is located 1.5 kilometers south of Tyre. The French government originally built it in 1939 for Armenian refugees. Palestinians from the Acre area in Galilee came to El-Buss in the 1950s after the *Nakbah*, and the Armenians were moved to the Anja area. Because of its relatively small size and its location, the camp was spared much of the violence that other camps experienced throughout the Lebanese civil war. The residents of El-Buss generally work in seasonal agricultural and construction. In addition, UNRWA reports that Palestinians live in concrete block shelters that they built for themselves. The water, sewerage, and storm water systems were rehabilitated between 2007 and 2008.

Finally, Rashidieh camp is divided into "old" and "new" sections. The French built the older part of the camp in 1936 to accommodate Armenian refugees that fled to Lebanon in 1936. In 1963, UNRWA built the new section to accommodate Palestinian refugees who were evacuated from a temporary camp called Gouraud camp in the Baalbek area of Lebanon. Most of the inhabitants of Rashidieh camp originally come from Deir al-Qassi, Alma an-Naher, and other villages in northern Palestine. The camp lies on the coast, about five kilometers from Tyre. UNRWA reported that Rashidieh was heavily affected during the Lebanese civil war, especially between 1982 and 1987. Nearly six hundred shelters were totally or partially destroyed and more than five thousand refugees were displaced. Remaining shelters needed serious rehabilitation. In addition, employment opportunities are very limited. Most residents work seasonally in agriculture and construction. Variations across the seven camps I visited in Jordan and Lebanon permitted me to trace the different strategies Palestinian refugees used to find protection through property rights.

INTERVIEW SAMPLING AND LIMITING BIAS

After I selected camps, I developed a set of interview questions that assessed how Palestinians arrived in the camps, how they build homes and/or businesses, and how they responded to the political and economic changes they confronted. The bulk of data for this book was collected during four research trips in the summer of 2004, the summer of 2005, the spring and summer of 2007, and the summer of 2012.

I used semi-structured interviews. This means a set list of questions was prepared, but many of the questions were open ended and naturally led to new questions that could not have been predicted prior to the interview. Conducting solid field research is a learning process, and the questions I asked in interviews reflected this process. Notably, the set of interview questions evolved between my first research trip in 2004 and my last visit in 2012, though the general direction of the questions remained the same. My questions in 2004 focused on basic facts in the camps as I sought to generate a complete picture of the refugee camps, the landscape of the market, the variety of business sectors, and the basic political dynamics. As I gained more experience and a better understanding of the theoretical literature and facts on the ground, I lengthened my list of questions. Moreover, I was able to ask questions that better accounted for the processes of property rights formation during interviews in 2005, 2007, and 2012. Appendix B contains my various interview scripts.

I did my best to keep questions consistent across camps. Interviews were conducted in Arabic. I wrote down interview responses by hand. To preserve the reliability of interview respondents, an interview assistant accompanied me and wrote down responses. This meant that I had two transcripts from each interview. Due to concerns for the privacy and protection of my interviewees, interviews were not tape recorded and anonymity was guarded. This was also a requirement of the Institutional Review Board (IRB) of ethics for interviewing human subjects. To attribute a particular comment to an interviewee and still protect their identity, I designate a number and letter that correspond to a list of interviewees with the date, location, and general occupation of a respondent in appendix B. For example, I-1L indicates the first interview conducted in Lebanon. If a J follows a number, it designates an interview in Jordan.

I administered interview questions to Palestinians using nonrandom snowball sampling methods. After I arrived in a camp, I hit the pavement and created a tally of different types of community members. For example, I sought out business owners, members of

camp committee offices, local camp historians, legal experts, lawyer, religious elders, and older as well as younger residents. I would
approach a resident and ask if they would like to talk. I emphasized
that I wanted to hear their story. Most Palestinians were puzzled by
my interest in them. In fact, one man said, "Are you sure you want
to talk to me? I am nobody special. I have no *wasta*, or political connection." I insisted that he was exactly the kind of person that I
needed to interview and that his voice mattered to me. There was a
97.9 percent response rate. After an interview, I asked if the respondent would be willing to introduce me to other people to interview.
Through these introductions, I slowly built up my list of interviewees. Notably, this type of method can introduce sampling bias, where
I might receive only a sliver of the total story of how the camps protected themselves through property rights. Perhaps interviews with
particular groups of residents skewed the camp narrative in a particular direction.

In order to limit bias, I used a couple of techniques. First, I interviewed as many different people as I possibly could, even (and especially) people who disagreed with one another. I interviewed people
from a variety of political leanings, small and large business owners, nongovernmental organizations, UNRWA officials, technical
experts, academics, and families. Findings tended to be consistent
across interviewees. Second, I interviewed most refugees on several
occasions over the course of many years. I felt that if I was getting
a similar story over time, then it was more likely that the responses
were true and not due to the refugee's mood on one particular day.
In addition, I used data triangulation methods to get a cohesive
story. For example, I used UNRWA archival images, copies of property titles saved in committee offices, and my own personal obser-
vations to back up the claims. Using these strategies, I limited bias to
the best of my abilities.

Ultimately, I conducted two hundred interviews in Jordan and
Lebanon. The conversations with Palestinian refugees provide a
rich and detailed narrative of how the community found protection
through property rights in a transitional landscape. Their insights

shed light on the power of existing theories of institutional formation. Whenever possible, I use the refugee's own accounts to trace
the pathway to property rights formation.

When you reach the end of this book, you should take away five key
contributions from this study. First, the Palestinian voice provides
a rich tapestry of everyday life in a refugee camp. Palestinians, far
from being passive in accepting their marginal political economic
status in the world, were actively engaging with their environment
and devising strategies for creating order out of chaos.

Second, property rights were one tool that Palestinians used to
find protection in a transitional space. Interestingly, property rights
protected financial assets and the community from incorporation
into states and outside political groups that sought to dominate them.

Third, Palestinians deployed dynamic strategies that fit their
particular circumstances to build property rights. Early on, they
developed rules that drew upon pre-1948 ways of doing business,
claiming assets, and enforcement that were easily replicable in the
camps without state intervention. Later, they strategically melded
their own interests with those of outside groups to protect the community from predation.

Fourth, the formalization of property rights yielded unintended
consequences for the community seeking protection. There was
a tension between the protections that property rights offered to
everyday residents and the submission to outsider authority when
Palestinians brokered agreements with the Jordanian government,
the Lebanese military, and Fatah in the later years in the camps. The
Palestinian case highlights the delicate balance between protection
and subjugation during the formalization of property rights.

Finally, the successes and failures of Palestinian refugees in Jordan
and Lebanon provide transportable lessons to the vast number of
communities living in transitional settings around the world today.

2

CRAFTING INFORMAL PROPERTY RIGHTS IN *FAWDAH*

In the beginning, everything was fawdah [chaos].

—I-8L

CHAOS AFTER THE NAKBAH

The most common word that Palestinians used to describe early life in the refugee camps was *fawdah,* meaning chaos or anarchy. After the disaster of the 1948 war, Palestinians were thrust into unfamiliar surroundings in host countries strewn across the Middle East. Besides meeting the most basic human needs, aid organizations or host states provided little support in governing the camps. A purposeful "protection gap" meant that Palestinians had to transition from rural Palestinian villages to refugee camp life on their own. A cinderblock and tile manufacturer described the early transition: "We started from scratch in the camps. There was nothing. We pulled ourselves out of the dirt" (I-28L).

In the midst of the chaos, Palestinians created order through informal property rights. These rules protected their belongings and preserved their community. I begin by tracing how Palestinians were treated upon their arrival in host countries and how UNRWA brokered camp agreements with Jordan and Lebanon. To create a holistic picture of the early years, I use historical accounts, scholarly articles, UNRWA information sheets, and interview data. The early years of chaos that resulted from the protection gap created similar pathways to informal property rights formation in Jordan and Lebanon. As a result, I pool interview data on the initial years following the *Nakbah* in camps across Jordan and Lebanon.

Initially, Palestinian villages tried to resolve the chaos through violent clashes. However, early camp battles were not productive and led to increasing disharmony because no single Palestinian village could claim victory and dominate the camps. At the same time, entrepreneurial Palestinians were slowly growing small businesses. In this climate, Palestinians felt they had no other choice than to adopt a system of property rights that established order. In interviews, Palestinians said they overcame disunity and borrowed from pre-1948 village templates of property ownership experienced under Ottoman and British rule to meet challenges in the camps.

Though Palestinians had myriad traditions from which to borrow and inform their system of rules in camps across Jordan and Lebanon, they strategically chose experiences that emphasized the *ahl* (family) or *hamula* (tribe) as the primary organizing unit in the camps and village norms of honor and *'ayb* (shame) to enforce informal property claims when there was no state to govern. Across camps, informal property rights evolved organically and in a manner similar to some of the expectations of the spontaneous order theory of institutional formation. Informal property rights were far from perfect, with unresolved property disputes turning into revenge schemes sometimes spiraling into violence among families. Still, informal property rights did offer a measure of asset protection and buffered the community from co-optation by powerful outsiders in a transitional space.

PALESTINIANS IN JORDAN

Jordan's initial response to the influx of Palestinian refugees reflected local conditions in the nascent Hashemite monarchy. Jordan was an artificial imperial creation carved out by British and Western powers. Jordan's leaders sought to tame and control disparate Bedouin and regional factions. King Abdallah I worked tirelessly to co-opt factions and consolidate his regime. Historians describe the difficult challenges that Jordan's kings faced because of their historical roots. For example, "King Hussein was fundamentally and structurally a client king . . . for all practical purposes the Hashemite legacy inherited from his grandfather was one of continuing dependence on the West" (Shlaim 2008, 154). Jordan was a poor country between 1949 and 1967. It had been desperately poor as the Amirate of Transjordan and the addition of Palestinians, half of who were refugees, aggravated the economic situation (Dann 1989, 11). British and American subsidies were essential components of the funding of the Hashemite state. Funds from UNRWA also helped balance the early state budget. In many ways, Jordan depended upon "Western handouts" for economic survival (Dann 1989, 11).

The drastic influx of Palestinian refugees in 1948 represented a pivotal strategic issue for Jordanian leadership. On one hand, Palestinians represented a potential source of destabilization. At the time, Jordan's estimated population ranged from 340,000 to 400,000 people. Following the *Nakbah* of 1948, the Jordanian-Palestinian Committee for the Study of Living Conditions of Refugees estimated that 506,200 or 55 percent of all Palestinian refugees fled to Jordan. Palestinian refugees caused the population of Jordan to triple within two short years. Even today, Jordan houses the largest number of Palestinian refugees in the Middle East. Coupled with the assassination of King Abdullah I in 1951 and the tumultuous transition to power among family members when King Hussein assumed the throne in 1953, Jordan's leadership was facing an uncertain political landscape.

On the other hand, consolidating power over the Palestinians could signal the strength and power of Jordan in domestic, regional, and international political arenas. Jordan offered Palestinians citizenship. However, their transitional community status remained despite these advances. Palestinians still faced limits on their employment activities and citizenship conferred very different meanings depending upon their year of arrival, place of origin, and political connections in Jordan. Edward Said describes a visit to Jordan in 1967 and explains the feeling most Palestinians had about Jordan at the time. He writes, "Yet, so far as I could tell—and this was certainly true for me—no one really felt at home in Amman, and yet no Palestinian could feel more at home anywhere else now" (Said 1994, 6).

To deal with the Palestinians, the Jordanian government developed a specific branch, linked to the Ministry of Foreign Affairs, to be in charge of dealing with Palestinian refugees (www.dpa.gov.jo/). This branch, known today as the Department of Palestinian Affairs (DPA), has had a variety of names over the decades but has fulfilled the same functions. Initially, the DPA was known as the Ministry of Refugees and partnered with UNRWA. It dealt with issues like the establishment of suitable plots of land for the camps, the issuance of legal identification documents, and the provision of basic humanitarian needs. From 1951 to 1967, the DPA was called the Ministry of Construction and Restoration, and the organization at the time focused on the improvement of physical conditions in the camps (www.dpa.gov.jo/). From 1967 to 1971 the DPA was known as the High Ministerial Council (www.dpa.gov.jo/).

For Palestinians, early life in Jordan was difficult and reflective of a transitional political landscape:

> Most of us arrived with nothing. We had no way to earn a living. Almost all of us were farmers that now lived in a cramped urban spot. Everyday, just to get enough food and water was difficult. And people think of Jordan as a warm desert. Hah! But at night and during the winter months it was freezing cold and snowed. We focused on creating a better home to stay warm. (I-2J)

"The basic struggle was simply to survive, political organizing or activity was a luxury few could afford" (Gubser 1983, 15). Palestinian refugees in Jordan worked to cobble together an existence. After visiting camps in Jordan in 1964, the UNRWA commissioner-general reported that "a large part of the refugee community is still living today in dire poverty, often under pathetic and in some cases appalling conditions" (Brand 1988, 153).

In sum, the early decades in Palestinian refugee camps were very difficult for the community to thrive. Though Jordan developed a system to deal with the basic needs of Palestinians, the refugee camps still represented a transitional space with serious protection gaps that had little support on issues of governance.

PALESTINIANS IN LEBANON

In Lebanon, conditions were extremely challenging for Palestinians. Lebanon was ill-prepared to handle the initial influx of Palestinians in 1948 when the *Nakbah* or the catastrophic 1948 war created the refugee situation (Schiff 1993). Many have characterized the Lebanese state as a "reluctant host" to Palestinian refugees since 1948 (Knudsen 2009). In this capacity, the Lebanese state sought to prevent the permanent integration and settlement of Palestinians in the country. The state structure strategically isolated the Palestinian community, creating a transitional political economic space. They created purposeful protection gaps that denied Palestinians many basic rights and placed them in "legal limbo" (Knudsen 2009). One refugee camp leader described the camps as "isolated islands" swimming in a Lebanese ocean (I-26L).

The early years were impossibly hard. A Palestinian refugee that walked to Lebanon in 1948 and grew up in the camps recalled what life was like for his family:

My mother contracted an easily preventable disease, tetanus, and died in the camp of a horrible death. My father was broken after he lost everything in Palestine because he had no future as a farmer in the refugee camp. I remember feeling hungry all the time. There were seven kids in our family to feed. Once, I recall my family had run out of pita bread. There was not a morsel of food in the house. Not having even a single piece of bread was a desperate sign. I was so worried and starving. God must have been watching out for us on that day, because I was walking and praying and, suddenly, I found a Lebanese coin on the ground. I took it to the falafel shop and bought fresh hot falafel, hummus, and bread for my family. We all got to eat! It was a rare feast. Somehow we survived those times. (I-96L)

Lebanon was neither socially nor politically welcoming of Palestinian refugees. Host country policy laid the foundation for a transitional Palestinian space. Lebanese citizens believed the presence of Palestinians upset the delicate balance among religious sects in their confessional political system. In this type of political system, each religious group is designated a number of parliamentary seats based on their demographic representation. The influx of Sunni Palestinians would disrupt a fragile political compromise.

In particular, the Palestinian situation in Lebanon was marked by a refusal of *tawtin*, or resettlement.[1] In national surveys, an overwhelming percentage of the Lebanese population, regardless of sectarian affiliation, refused *tawtin* for Palestinians. In one survey, 87 percent of Maronites, 78 percent of Shiites, 78 percent of Catholics, 78 percent of orthodox, 71 percent of Druze, and 63 percent of Sunnis in Lebanon opposed *tawtin* (Sayigh 1995). These surveys indicate that Lebanese citizens disagreed with Palestinian resettlement or integration into broader Lebanese society.

Aside from informal social isolation, Lebanon codified their desire for the legal isolation of Palestinian refugees through work restrictions and impositions against property ownership outside the refugee camps. Palestinians in Lebanon, unlike those living Jordan, were not issued passports. They could sometimes attain laissez-passer travel documents, but these were difficult to access in many circumstances. In addition to limitations on travel within and outside the country, Lebanon's 1964 and 1995 laws outlined the rights and responsibilities of foreigners to live and work in Lebanon, identifying Palestinians as a special case independent of the treatment of most foreign nationals. For example, in Lebanon, Palestinians are banned from seventy professions. One commentator wondered, "Can you imagine a Palestinian refugee family who has lived in Lebanon for over 50 years without the right to work?" (Christoff 2004). In addition, a 2002 law forbade Palestinians from owning land or buying property in Lebanon (Christoff 2004). In effect, Palestinian refugee camps occupied a transitional space that legally isolated them from formal state structures in Lebanon.

UNRWA BROKERED REFUGEE CAMPS

Host countries and international aid organizations scrambled to accommodate Palestinian refugees after 1948. The Red Cross was the first to administer aid to Palestinians (I-91L). Once UNRWA was established, it took over the task of providing assistance to Palestinian refugees. Though UNRWA was mandated with this power, Palestinians were weary of UNRWA's motives and activities. After all, many Palestinians felt that it was the UN partition of Palestine that was partially responsible for their displacement in the first place (I-91L). In this precarious context, UNRWA acted as the primary broker and welfare advocate for the Palestinian people in Lebanon and Jordan. "UNRWA brokered humanitarian agreements with host country governments to allocate land for Palestinian refugee use" (I-3J, I-21L). This agreement was revised in 1967 to accommodate the influx of Palestinians who fled Gaza following the Arab defeat in the 1967 Arab-Israeli War (I-3J, I-2L).

UNRWA's public information officer in Jordan noted, "The land was given from the Hashemite Kingdom to UNRWA. It is not clear how Jordan procured the land for Palestinian use but when UNRWA was given it, it was responsible for providing it, and other services like health, welfare, and education to Palestinian refugees" (I-3J).

Additionally, UNRWA's public information officer in Lebanon stated, "UNRWA contracted with the Lebanese to find suitable land for Palestinians. Host countries played no role in how the land was divided up for Palestinian use" (I-21J).

Lebanon agreed to lease land to UNRWA for Palestinian use for ninety-nine years, but the host country absolved itself of any role in the division and use of land among refugees (I-3J, I-21L). Some land allocated for Palestinian use was also on indefinite loan from religious institutions and private families (Roberts 2010, 77). In over one hundred interviews in Lebanon, there was never a clear understanding of who originally owned the land that camps occupy or what the ninety-nine-year lease agreement meant for the host country and the refugee population in the long term. Other experts of Palestinian refugee camps in Lebanon and Jordan agree that the policy is ambiguous and complex. Though some characterize the ambiguity of the land agreement as a disadvantage for Palestinians, the political ambiguity of this space also provides for opportunity (Roberts 2010). The ambiguity advantaged Palestinians because it gave them the freedom to develop institutions of protection that reflected their community needs.

Refugee camps in Jordan and Lebanon were set up on small areas of uncultivated land or on abandoned military campsites formerly occupied by colonial armies. Conditions were "primitive in the extreme" up until the early 1950s (Sirhan 1975). Over time, sand and earth were covered by cement and tents gave way to shacks that were eventually replaced by cement block homes. Gradually, latrines were replaced by private installations. Originally, UNRWA supplied water through tankers. Only 35 percent of homes in the camps had electricity and only 40 percent of homes had running water by the late 1960s (Sirhan 1975). Camps have roughly remained the same size since their inception, but population growth has continued unabated. As a result, there is a high population density in the camps.

At first, UNRWA adopted the role of allocating resources, like land, to Palestinian refugees. UNRWA allotted each family a plot of land and a tent based on the number of family members in each grouping (I-2J, I-3J, I-2L, I-3L, I-21L, I-29L). For example, every six to eight family members received a tent and small plot of land (I-2J, I-3J, I-2L, I-3L, I-21L, I-29L). An UNRWA officer explained the early arrangements with Palestinian refugees:

> Families received one tent apiece. Huge families of more than eight members were given second tents. They were assigned a plot of land and the spot was registered with their corresponding family registration number. After three or four years people fenced in the plots. By the mid-1950s, the agency [UNRWA] replaced tents with shelters or huts. The rooms were covered with sheeting materials for roofing. (I-3J)

Refugee camps looked like large tented fields that were filled with thousands of Palestinians living impossibly close to one another. Single-family tents were called "bell tents" because they were shaped like a bell (I-91L). Larger families often lived in "Indian" tents that looked like Native American teepees (I-91L). In addition, medical and school tents resembled the shapes of "circus" tents and were set up to provide basic services to residents (I-91L). A Palestinian man that grew up in Nahr al-Bared in the early 1950s fondly recalled windy days in the camps. "When I was a child I thought windy days were the best. A big gust would pick up and topple our school tent! The teacher would be so mad and sand would be kicked up everywhere. He would dismiss us early because there was nowhere for him to teach until the tent was put up again. I could go and play instead of study" (I-96L).

UNRWA held a lot of authority in the initial distribution of resources inside the camps, but the organization held an explicit policy of not interfering with the informal transfer of resources among refugees (I-3J). One UNRWA representative commented that "we didn't play politics inside the camps, we just helped to provide Palestinians with services. What they decided to do with them [land, food, water] was up to them" (I-5L). Another said, "Palestinians were given the right to use the land inside the refugee camps and develop it in the way they saw fit without UNRWA, host country, or local political interference" (I-21L). In Jordan, a public information officer said, "UNRWA is not a government and the refugees are not our subjects" (I-3J).

Palestinians were left to create order and find protection in the camps because host countries and UNRWA absolved themselves of any role in governing the camps. Though no one expected the refugee crisis to continue for as long as it has, the protection gap ultimately gave Palestinians a new lease on life. Palestinians could seize the opportunity to develop the dirt they now occupied. Palestinian communities could build homes, establish businesses, create plumbing and sewage systems, and establish electrical systems in what was otherwise a barren landscape inside the camps. Of course, none of these innovations happened immediately.

COMMUNAL TENSION AFTER *NAKBAH*

Initially, Palestinians tried to resolve the chaos through forceful and violent encounters between competing villages thrust together in the camps. Palestinians attempted to establish order through violence and might. Umbeck's study of the California gold rush found that claims to valuable resources were established and protected through an individual's ability to forcefully maintain exclusivity (1981, 39). Force or the use of violence served as a key tool to determine the initial distribution and protection of assets in the American "wild, wild West" (Umbeck 1981). In Palestinian refugee camps, this initial effort at establishing order through violent conflict was thwarted because no village was armed or powerful enough to establish dominance and maintain exclusive access to resources over the rest of the villages.

In Lebanon and Jordan, Palestinian refugee camps were grouped around pre-1948 villages. Old village dynamics and patterns of interaction were reproduced in the camps. "In this way many villages

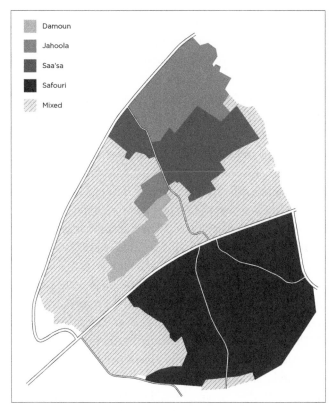

MAP 2.1 Pre-1948 Palestinian villages were kept intact in Nahr al-Bared refugee camp. This map was adapted from a UNRWA map.

which the Israelis occupied, evacuated, and demolished in Palestine are still, socially speaking, alive and coherent units" (Sirhan 1975, 102). They have lost neither their social consciousness nor their family and village ties. The map of neighborhoods based on pre-1948 village origins depicts the communal geography in NBC camp in Lebanon. This official UNRWA document, created in 2007 to map pre-1948 villages in the camps, represents the patterns of groupings present in other camps. It shows that communities stuck together after 1948 for better or worse.

Though social cohesion is evident based on the physical structure of the camps, social conflict was not absent at the family or village level inside the camps. Old family and village feuds carried over into the camps. One resident summarized the early disharmony: "In the early years of chaos, there were conflicts over water usage, tent placement, tent size, divorces, and marriage matches" (I-91L).

These small conflicts sparked larger intra-camp battles. Villages sought to dominate each other and establish order in the camps. Camps historians in Lebanon and Jordan described the initial difficulty of agrarian communities moving to urban and congested living conditions with strangers from different villages. Initially, refugees did not feel that the refugee camp resembled a real community (I-91L). In the early 1950s, there was a lot of "social stress" among relocated Palestinian villages that were forced to live together in the same refugee camp (I-91L).

For example, different villages sought to dominate the camp. This prompted an internal camp "war" between the larger Safouri village and the smaller Saa'sa Palestinian village over land and space in NBC (I-91L). There were three battles along the shoreline of the camp. During battle, different villages were identified by the style of pantaloons or underpants that women wore into battle while fighting alongside men (I-91L). "Women would use their long skirts to carry rocks that family members would throw. Women with bell-shaped pantaloons came from Saa'sa village and women with tapered pantaloons were from the opposing village" (I-91L).

During battle, the women of Saa'sa chanted, "Oh, the One that helps the six beat sixty; give victory to the ones with the underpants like us!" Despite the three battles, there was no decisive victor and intra-camp relations were strained from the unrest (I-91L). Again, Umbeck's (1981) theory of the formation of property rights through violence did not work in the refugee camps because no group was powerful enough to maintain exclusivity. There were similar intra-camp conflicts all over Jordan and Lebanon. The absence of a clear victor created even more disharmony and chaos for camp residents. In the case of the Palestinian refugee camps, the historical record suggests that there was roughly an equal distribution of power such that no single Palestinian village was powerful enough to dominate camp life and bring order to the community. This peculiarity of the community made it possible for a shared vision of property management to emerge rather than a model imposed by a powerful ruling family or village. A camp resident noted, "We learned that fighting with one another was not going to solve our problems" (I-24L). As time progressed, refugees agreed that a new model of community governance and protection should develop. A chief UNRWA information officer noted, "Initially there was conflict. In the course of time, it [the camp] turned into neighborhoods" (I-3J).

"CREATING GOLD" THROUGH HARD EFFORT

At the same time that the community realized violence would not create order in the camps, entrepreneurial Palestinians worked hard to grow their businesses in the difficult conditions of camp life. Young Palestinian men looked to the Gulf countries as a golden opportunity to earn money and build a better life for themselves and their families back in the camps (Brand 1988; Rubenberg 1983). In fact, Ghassan Kanafani's famous short story "Men in the Sun" highlights the arduous desert journey and extreme lengths, including risking one's own life, to which Palestinian men would go to make it to the Gulf. There was a strong communal norm that young Palestinian men working abroad would send the majority of their earned income to family members living inside the camps. Most young Palestinian men shared cramped apartments in the Gulf and Libya for many years to save money for their families. During interviews, business owners said that housing and building improvements were primarily financed by remittances sent by family members that worked in the Gulf or Libya. Residents revealed that the number one source of capital for investment came from remittance flows. Remittances gave Palestinian refugees the capital necessary to invest in a variety of camp resources. For example, an iron welder in Beddawi noted that he began his business in 1972 (I-11L). He earned the money to start the business by working in Libya for ten years from 1962 to 1972, where he also learned to weld and work with iron. When he returned to the camp, he used his remittance savings to marry, begin a family, and set up his iron welding and design business inside Beddawi. This pathway to business development was a common pattern in interviews.

Indeed, remittances were more important than UNRWA or Islamic bank loans in starting businesses (I-11L). Though such loans were theoretically available to Palestinian refugees, budget constraints and the high demand for loans made it impossible for most businesses to rely on UNRWA (I-2L). As a result, "most of the money that permitted refugees to initially invest in their homes and business in the camps came from remittances sent by family members" (I-2L).

The influx of money from remittances caused a surge in the demand for building supplies because people could finally afford to improve their tents to more permanent homes, as well as open businesses. Many refugees opened businesses on the bottom floor of their tent plot and then built homes above the stores (I-3J, I-21L). "Slowly, refugees demolished their huts and built new and better homes at their own expense" (I-3J). The typical refugee home sandwiches businesses with multigenerational levels of apartments extending upward. Usually the patriarch of the family lives directly above the store with his sons and their families occupying upper levels. It is not uncommon to find one small plot of land with a business on the ground level and four or five levels of apartment homes above it. Images of the camps today illustrate the texture of business growth in camps in Lebanon and Jordan. They depict the bustling markets filled with homes stretching upward and tangled wires powering progress in the camps.

In interviews, business owners said hard work was essential for their entrepreneurial success in a transitional space. "We have lived in dirt. But Palestinians knew that if we dug deep enough in the dirt, we would find gold. Our efforts created gold" (I-35J). In fact, the refugee economy became a central marketplace for neighboring Lebanese and Jordanian villagers to do business. The development of the Palestinian economy was quite remarkable given the dwindling aid and international assistance as the refugee situation persisted. The longer the protracted situation persisted, the more the overall budget for humanitarian aid assistance was repeatedly cut (Jacobsen 2005). With reduced aid, refugees had to create their own institutions to support themselves.

It is important to note that Palestinian refugees are not alone in their ability to create prosperity in a transitional space. There are many examples worldwide of refugee camps developing black market economies by selling humanitarian aid rations, engaging in small-scale enterprises, and working in the informal sector. For example, a study of the Kyangwali refugee settlement in Uganda noted that refugees achieved remarkable growth because of agricultural production, wage labor, small businesses, lending or investment schemes, and the trade of humanitarian rations (Werker 2007). Despite isolationist host country policies, refugees often traded non-food aid items such as clothes, household items, and construction materials at the local market for a profit. Refugees can sometimes get higher prices for "imported aid" products and can purchase cheaper local goods to replace the aid. In Semabkouya camp in Guinea, "Refugee small businesses get their start at the market by selling non-food items, particularly pots and blankets, as well as food rations. A full pot set and plates can bring as much as 18,000 GF. Replacement pots can be bought for as little as 9,000 GF, so this leaves a sufficient amount to invest in a new business" (Jacobsen 2005, 28).

Growth in the Palestinian refugee camps was assessed in several ways. For example, businesses were asked to provide basic information about the size and scope of their industry. A series of questions assessed industries in the camps: "What type of capital investments do you have?" "How many employees do you have (part-time and full-time)?" "Where do you do business or sell your products?"

The average business in Palestinian refugee camps across Lebanon and Jordan had at least three full-time employees other than the owner. Most businesses had part-time and seasonal laborers during busy times of the year. Construction business owners in the steel, tile, cement, carpentry, and glass businesses said they could hardly keep up with orders in the summer months. In addition, most owners had between $5,000 and $35,000 in personal capital investments in their businesses. In NBC and Beddawi camps, refugees also did business with clients outside the camps in the northern region of Lebanon. Some businesses even contracted with clients in Beirut. In Jordan, refugee businesses often did business with neighboring Jordanian markets. One respondent said, "For example, in Baqa'a camp there are roughly 86,000 people. There are lots of shops too, maybe 1,000 or 2,000. UNRWA had nothing to do with it. Neither did Jordan. They [the Palestinians] formed it on their own" (I-2J). Another said, "Businesses in Jordan were initially mom and pop style. They were rudimentary. But over time they evolved" (I-3J). Though navigating the markets was hard, most refugee businessmen agreed that "business was pretty good, even as a refugee" (I-2J).

A DYNAMIC RESPONSE TO CHAOS

Despite the increasing wealth inside the camps, there was still no system of order to protect community assets. An ice cream cone manufacturer said, "There was no organization inside the camps, especially for businesses. Everyone is his own boss. It was *fawdah* (anarchy). We needed a government to organize us" (I-8L).

UNRWA, Jordanian, and Lebanese policies of not governing the camps meant there was no government to create order inside the camps (I-3J). Moreover, attempts by villagers inside the camps to dominate through violence or force had proved ineffective. New Institutionalists might have predicted that Palestinians would have given up and gotten "locked into" the conditions of despair inside the camps because there was no credible third-party enforcer to build property rights.

But Palestinians were not paralyzed by the chaos and despair inside the camps. As Thelen (2004) suggests, individuals respond to conditions on the ground and readjust or shift their behavior when building institutions. Graeber (2004) reiterated this point when he noted that groups living in anarchy would push for institutions that govern their community within the constraints of their older experiences and possibilities of their new conditions. They would work to protect the community from outside domination and chaos while maintaining their group identity (7). In *Governing Gaza*, Feldman (2008) identifies the ways in which Gazans found order even in the absence of a legal sovereign power, especially when it was a stateless region from 1948 to 1967. For example, she asserts that the daily mundane work of bureaucrats issuing rations, pushing paper, and serving basic needs kept stability during the periods in between new regime rules. She says that the "reiterative authority" of bureaucrats reproducing titles, documents, or mundane tasks for the Gazan community created a measure of order when there was no legitimate sovereign power (Feldman 2008, 16–17). It is the everyday work of everyday people who functioned in disaster to create stability and rule in Gaza.

Similarly, Palestinian refugees responded dynamically to shifting conditions inside the camps. They functioned in disaster in an effort to craft order in anarchy. Nascent business entrepreneurs and everyday camp residents looked for ways to bring order to the chaos. A chocolate factory owner described the transition from chaos to order through property rights: "Over time my business grew. I was selling chocolate all the way up to Beirut. I had set up a good market. The camps also settled down too with less violence. And I believe the American saying is true, 'necessity is the mother of invention.' So Palestinians created a system of order on our own" (I-12L). Another resident in Jordan said, "The hard conditions challenged us everyday. We were forced to be creative and create a system that worked for us" (I-4J). A teacher emphasized that "Palestinians were empowered to do for themselves. No one else will do it for us" (I-20L).

The informal system of property rights developed organically in the camps. For example, some refugees were able to save up enough money to rent homes in nearby villages, so they sold or gave UNRWA-allocated land plots to their *ahl* or family members left inside the camps (I-3J, I-21L, I-47L).[2] In an informal manner, refugees bought, sold, and traded land plots with one another in Lebanon and Jordan (I-3J, I-47L). Refugees usually transferred property claims to their *ahl* through verbal or oral agreements with other refugees (I-3J, I-21L, I-47L). Sometimes religious officials and family elders witnessed the oral agreements (I-47L). In the event of a conflict over ownership, they went to religious officials or visited the family to resolve the dispute. One refugee summarized how the system of informal property rights functioned: "There were no lines demarcating the homes and businesses on a map. They were invisible. But it was understood that there was a distinction between where ownership began and ended" (I-3J).

In interviews, I searched for the specific time when property rights emerged in the camps. I probed for a magical moment when the community gathered and agreed to a system of rules that would govern the ownership of assets in their camps. Through interviews I learned that there was no exact moment or specific date when a system of rules emerged. It was a nonevent. As Sugden (1989) asserts in his description of the spontaneous order of institutional formation, it is a rare thing for a community to gather and collectively decide rules of ownership for driftwood on a beach where people collect wood. He reminds us that one does not normally see two cars pull aside, confer, and then come to a decision on who gets to traverse a one-lane bridge first. According to Sugden (1989), rules pop up when they are needed. Moreover, rules that are easy to replicate, regardless of conditions on the ground, are more likely to emerge as well. They can develop consciously or subconsciously as the community pushes for order and protection.

CONVERTING PRE-1948 PRACTICES INTO INFORMAL PROPERTY RIGHTS

Sugden (1989) and other spontaneous order scholars assume that property rights will naturally develop around valuable resources because of a static body of shared group history in managing property rights. However, communities living in transitional settings face significant hurdles in organically developing informal property rights around valuable resources. Specifically, Palestinians from different villages were thrust into the same cramped refugee camps and forced to live together. There were lots of conflicts. Moreover, different communities had myriad historical experiences and village values or norms with respect to land tenure practices to draw upon. What parts of their group history could Palestinians use to inform the functioning of the informal property rights system in refugee camps across Jordan and Lebanon?

Under Ottoman rule, there were a variety of ways in which Palestinians could "own" property. Unfortunately, Western scholars and political activists (both Palestinian and Israeli) often used their own legal terminology to analyze practices in Palestine prior to the *Nakbah*. This has led many to erroneously claim "that at the date of the partition of Palestine (1947) 'over 70 percent' of it [Palestine] did not 'legally' belong to the local Arab population but to the British mandated power" (Kemal 2014, 231). Based on such an argument, it would seem unlikely for Palestinians in the refugee camps to have any experience in owning property. According to Kemal's (2014) historical study of property ownership in Palestine, Palestinians did in fact have diverse experiences in land tenure practices.

The misleading interpretation of land tenure practices prior to the *Nakbah* ignored traditions of the local population and the complex system of property ownership during Ottoman rule. Up until 1858, there was no obligation for Palestinians to register property claims with Ottomans (Kemal 2014, 231). Until that time, there were a variety of ways property could be classified. First, *mulk* permitted owners to benefit from the possession and use of an asset. It was the closest notion to "private property" in the Western conception of the term. Deeds were usually registered in Islamic religious courts. This classification of property was usually found in urban city areas like inside the walls of Jerusalem. It was rare to discover areas of land considered *mulk* in rural areas. British studies of Palestine during the mandate era found *mulk* classifications to be "negligible" (Kemal 2014, 232). In contrast, 90 percent of the surface area of the Ottoman Empire was owned by the state (*miri*) and distributed for usufructure (*tassaruf*) in exchange for a tax on production. As such, *miri* property was not "privately owned" in the Western sense, but it was not "state-owned land" in the Western sense either because families that cultivated the land could sell their usufructury rights and pass those rights to their children. "State land, in the modern sense, is land that the state wishes to keep out of individual use, such as forest land. Such a legal category did not exist in the Ottoman Empire and came into being only in the new states. *Miri* land was not state land in this sense. There was never really a question of usurpation of such land; at the most it could be misused" (Kemal 2014, 232–33).

Furthermore, there were many areas of land that were classified as *miri* but designated as collective land holdings or *musha* to tribes, large families, and villages. "On the eve of the First World War it is estimated that around 70 percent of agricultural land in Palestine fell under this [*musha*] category" (Kemal 2014, 233). Families shared ownership of *musha* land in rotation with the village. The rotation in ownership might occur every one, two, or five years so that every farmer would have a chance to cultivate fertile land (Kemal 2014, 233). There were other categories of land holding like *waqf*, in which property was managed by pious Islamic foundations and used for the Muslim community. These lands fell outside the jurisdiction of Ottoman rule. In addition, there was *mawat* land that was owned by the state but not cultivated. It was considered "dead" land that was not suited for cultivation and was located far away from villages.

Often this land was used for grazing purposes (Kemal 2014, 233–34). Many historians argue that this land was probably "owned" by Bedouin communities. In addition, there was *matruka* land designated for public use. It could be used for roads, irrigation canals, rivers, or forests. Finally, there was *jiftlik* land located in the Jordan Valley that was held in the name of the Ottoman sultan. Suffice it to say that there was a complex entanglement of Ottoman and local cultural understandings of land ownership practices that Palestinian refugees could draw upon. It is not immediately clear which set of rules or practices they would draw upon to face the chaotic conditions in the refugee camps.

In *Rediscovering Palestine: Merchants and Peasants in Jabal Nablus, 1700–1900*, Beshara Doumani (1995) traces patterns of land ownership and economic growth in Palestinian communities under Ottoman rule. Doumani (1995) asserts that Palestinians in the Jabal Nablus region were no stranger to commercial agriculture, proto-industrial production, sophisticated credit relations, and commercial networks. During Ottoman times, most agricultural land in Palestine was state owned or *miri*. However, Palestinians did have "usufruct right as long as they did not allow these lands to lie fallow for more than three years. The right of use had no time limit: the land could be and was passed down through inheritance for generations. In return for its use, [Palestinian] peasants paid taxes (such as *ushr*, or tithe) that were levied both in cash and kind, plus a whole range of exactions" (Doumani 1995, 156).

Doumani further points out that peasants treated these lands as though they owned them privately. Over the centuries, each *ahl* and *hamula* became identified with particular lands, which they treated as private property. Moreover, court cases registered in the eighteenth and nineteenth century show that "peasants of Jabal Nablus did indeed dispose of nominally state lands as if they were private property by mortgaging, renting, or selling their usufruct rights" (Doumani 1995, 157). For example, a court case from May 29, 1837, demonstrated how Palestinian peasants treated the property as if it were privately owned when they sold land to others:

> Today, Yusuf al-Asmar son of Abdullah al-Jabali from the village of Bayta appeared before the noble council. Being of sound mind and body he voluntary testified . . . that he ceded, evacuated, and lifted his hand from the piece of land located in Khirbat Balata . . . to the pride of honorable princes, Sulayman Afandi son of . . . Husayn Afandi Abd-al Hadi. [The latter] compensated him 700 piasters . . . and the aforementioned Yusuf Asmar gave permission to Sulayman Afandi to take over the piece of land. (Doumani 1995, 157–58)

After decades of Ottoman and British colonial rule, Palestinian refugees had complex understandings of how property ownership should and could be defined and enforced. This assertion is further supported by interview data that assess the historical origins and community knowledge of pre-*Nakbah* land ownership practices. I asked refugees to trace if and how historical experiences and religious values informed the practice of property ownership in the early years inside Palestinian refugee camps. In addition, the data highlight the desire for protection from elite predation and preservation of Palestinian identity among community members.

In interviews refugees were asked: "Did you own land, a home, or a business in Palestine? If yes, how did you claim ownership? Were you familiar with writing contracts or having documents that signified ownership before you arrived in the refugee camps?" In addition, refugees were invited to recount their family history of land ownership in Palestine. Every refugee interviewed had some sort of "proof" that they once owned land and farms in Palestine. A few had old titles outlining property ownership.

Though my interview data indicate that the majority of refugees felt they owned land in Palestine prior to 1948, there is significant disagreement over the actual percentage of refugees that "owned" land. In 1951, the United Nations Conciliation Commission for

Palestine (UNCCP) undertook a major study "to determine the scope and value of the property abandoned by Palestinian refugees in Israel" and to develop specific procedures for compensating refugee losses (Fischbach 2003, 114). John Berncastle, a British land expert, was tasked with leading the UNCCP study and estimated abandoned property based on British documentation of village statistics dating from 1945. Notably, he did not consult refugees in camps when he arrived at the number of abandoned properties. He found that 40 to 50 percent of Palestinian peasant land was not "owned" by the peasants themselves and likely belonged to elite Palestinians (Fischbach 2003). Taking this perspective, refugees had a very small claim of ownership in property in Palestine prior to 1948.

However, the historical record is more complicated than the UNCCP and Berncastle's findings. Sami Haddawi, "the premier Arab expert on land in Palestine" due to his extensive experience with the British Department of Land Settlement in Palestine from 1919 to 1927, floated much higher estimates of Palestinian ownership and losses (Fischbach 2003, 213). Haddawi believed British tax assessments were too low because at the time there were only four persons that actually inspected property for all of Palestine (Fischbach 2003, 214). Haddawi felt that they rarely did a careful and accurate assessment of land and capital. Izzat Tannous, another contemporary of Berncastle and Haddawi, operated the Arab Refugee Property Owners in Palestine and his organization suggested "impossibly high" figures of ownership (Fischbach 2003, 215). These examples indicate the conflicting and politicized "official" accounts of how much property Palestinian refugees owned. Though this debate is interesting, from the perspective of my study, whether or not Palestinian refugees really "owned" the land in the *Western sense* of the word is less important. It is most important that Palestinian refugees had experience buying, selling, and renting land or capital prior to 1948. Their pre-1948 experiences informed patterns of property ownership in the chaotic conditions of the refugee camps. In interviews, some refugees explained how their

village owned the land collectively as *musha* and how it was indi-
vidually cultivated:

> My family owned olive groves in Palestine. We lived in Samoie village
> close to the bigger city of Safad. We were a big family and we all lived
> close to each other. We had farmed this land for as long as anyone can
> remember in our family history. Before 1948, I can remember falling
> asleep as a boy to the sound of rumbles of the olives dropping onto
> ground during the harvest season. My Mom and the other women
> would press the olives together to make oil. She would also make
> olive soap for us to wash with. Some of the olives were preserved in
> oil for us to eat later on. I don't have a title today to show for it. We
> certainly "owned" it by Ottoman standards of *miri or musha* because
> we cultivated it. (I-96L)

Refugees also highlighted how they had been dispossessed from
their own land. For example, one resident said, "I have lived in the
camps for fifty six years, since 1948. I have the title to my home in
the camp. But my home is originally in Palestine, in a village called
Um-al-Faraj, near Aqaar in Palestine. I still have my documents that
show ownership of our home and farm there. It is important, even
until today. You need rules to keep you safe" (I-23L). "I have my keys
to my old home in Palestine. I also have the Ottoman document
showing what I owned in Palestine. I learned, long ago, that you
need to show you own your home for protection" (I-52L).

In summary, Palestinian refugees had a deep reservoir of
knowledge and experience in managing and defining ownership of property. In addition, they were comfortable operating
in ambiguous or, at the very least, confusing political economic
landscapes. Navigating the maze of Ottoman land tenure classifications, Ottoman courts, Islamic religious courts, and British
council administrators during the mandate era unexpectedly
prepared them for the chaos, legal ambiguity, and "protection
gap" they would confront in the Palestinian refugee camps across
Lebanon and Jordan.

STRATEGIC SELECTION OF PALESTINIAN PRACTICES

Given the myriad experiences Palestinians could draw upon to develop rules of ownership in the camps, how did Palestinians organically decide to manage property rights in an informal manner after their arrival in the refugee camps? In his study of stateless tribes, Scott finds that a shared identity, whether really shared or strategically crafted, became "the political structure of rule. . . . It became the recognized way to assert a claim to autonomy, resources, land, trade route, and any other valuable that required a state-like claim to sovereignty" (Scott 2009, 258–59). Again, whether or not these community histories were in fact really shared by the entire community or strategically developed accounts of pre-1948 life is unimportant. The ambiguity and porousness of the community's history was a political resource crafted to meet the challenges of life in a "fractured" or transitional zone (Scott 2009, 258). In the absence of a state and an established judicial system like the Ottoman courts, Palestinians resorted to pre-1948 community practices to informally govern property in the camps.

As a researcher, it was difficult for me to comprehend how Palestinians could not identify the exact moment they developed informal rules of ownership, thereby relegating rule adoption to the realm of spontaneous generation, and still discuss in interviews how certain pre-1948 village practices and values were carefully curated to meet the challenges of refugee camp life, thereby emphasizing the strategic choice behind rule adoption. Drawing upon the work of spontaneous order scholars, I believe one of the keys to understanding how rules organically *and* strategically developed is based on Sugden's (1989) discussion of the "ease of rule replicability" as the governing principle for norm adoption with respect to valuable assets. Sugden suggests that rules for defining and enforcing property will develop and persist if they are easy to put to use. Axelrod's (1984) study of the evolution of cooperation in simulated computer games emphasizes a similar notion of the evolutionary advantages for cooperation rather than conflict. Scott also picks up on this intellectual thread when he talks about the "adaptive value" of certain community behaviors. Over time, "as one identity became increasingly valuable and another less so," communities would be expected to adapt to the more valuable practice or identity (Scott 2009, 249). In summary, Palestinians tried a variety of strategies like the violent conflicts in the early refugee camps years, but found that pre-1948 community practices that emphasized cooperation through kinship and values of honor and shame were easier to use and therefore adopted.

Farsoun and Zacharia (1997) and Nadan (2006) identify pre-1948 Palestinian village practices for governing the rural economy during the Ottoman era and the British mandate period. He argues that patrilineal structures of kinship linked community members in real and imagined ways. These connections created the bedrock of community trust that governed political and economic transactions in the absence of a state or outside authority (Nadan 2006, 196). The central identifying patrilineal units of the Palestinian village were one's *ahl* or family and their *hamula*, a broader association embodying many families much like a patrilineal clan or tribe (Farsoun and Zacharia 1997, 23; Nadan 2006, 197). These units were both genealogical and imagined, meaning someone could be *like* a cousin or brother though not share blood lines. The *hamulas* regulated and guaranteed "access to productive lands and the rights of individuals over them" (Farsoun and Zacharia 1997, 23). In effect, if everyone could be your brother or cousin or potentially a second or third cousin through marriage, one would not dare to dishonor and shame the family in communal dealings over property ownership and protection. An old Arab proverb highlights this way of thinking: "Me and my brother against our cousin, and me and my cousin against the stranger." Patrilineal kinship ties anchored norms of behavior with respect to property ownership and conflict mediation. In sum, "patrilineal understandings [of ownership] were not signed in the manner of official contracts, as this would be regarded as shame or *'ayb*" (Nadan 2006, 196). The power of shame and honor in communities meant that informal handshakes were enough to enforce good behavior even in the absence of state authority.

For example, Nadan (2006) found that the Palestinian farmers or *fellahin* preferred to barter rather than push for cash transactions. "The village barber, for instance, was paid in kind for his services one a year at harvest time, and a carpenter would receive measures of wheat in return for maintenance of plows and for other work" (Nadan 2006, 174). Palestinians in the same community trusted that they would be paid, sometimes many months after an exchange, because they shared kinship ties.

Ahl and *hamulas* also protected individuals and kin during external conflicts. "Led by their own *sheiks* or religious leaders, the *hamulas* therefore provided the individual within the nuclear family collective protection in all aspects of his or her life," especially during times of transition with new regimes and imperial powers seeking dominance (Farsoun and Zacharia 1997, 23). These pre-1948 village practices indicate that Palestinian refugees in Lebanon and Jordan, mostly hailing from the same rural places Nadan (2006) and Faroun and Zacharia (1997) studied, would have an easily replicable blueprint of kinship ties that embedded notions of honor and shame to anchor transactions in the chaos of the refugee camps.

In interviews Palestinian refugees emphasized how pre-1948 community codes of behavior anchored the enforcement of property rights. The owner of a glass business in Baqa'a camp explained, "There are strong religious and community values that are very traditional here. It makes protection an easy thing for us" (I-12J). Another said, "I trust in God and my neighbors to protect my home and business" (I-47L). A carpenter in Baqa'a camp said, "I rarely encountered problems [stealing, expropriation] with my business in the camp because we have strong Palestinian values. It is shameful to your family if you did these things. Everyone would know your reputation was ruined if you behaved that way" (I-9J).

Though the system of property rights lacked a judicial system to enforce rules, the community adopted rules that emphasized values of honor and shame. They were easy to use because they required little physical infrastructure and planning to create or use. It simply required social policing or community vigilance. There were high reputational costs for one's family if one engaged in bad behavior that trampled on the property of others. A sheikh underscored the importance of a family's reputation inside the camps" "If one's family name was tarnished it influenced the ability of people to marry well and conduct future business in the area. A bad event had implications for future generations in your family" (I-79L). The power of informal rules was also emphasized in an interview with a Palestinian working for UNRWA: "If Nahr al-Bared camp were a Lebanese village, they would have much more crime. But they don't. They don't fight that much. It is because they have strong traditional values for protection" (I-5L).

Of course, like any community, there were communal conflicts and petty crimes, but for the most part refugees felt safe among their community in refugee camps because strong values of honor and shame anchored their communal behavior. Though Palestinians had many options to govern property in the camps, refugees adopted informal rules that emphasized community values that promoted cooperation through shared ideas of honor and shame. These rules were adopted because they were easy to put into practice in a transitional space.

The informal system of rules was far from perfect. Sometimes a transgression created an unending cycle of violence between families (I-79L). "Blood feuds could erupt when the community could not come to a solution over a problem" (I-79L). Informal rules could be terribly inefficient to enforce. At times "certain families were able to sway decisions in their favor compared with other less influential (or large) families" (I-54L). It is not my intention to present a utopian ideal of the early years in the camps. Far from it, the first couple of decades in the camps were messy and hard. They were filled with *fawdah* or chaos. Despite the difficulties,

Palestinian entrepreneurs slowly grew businesses and residents improved their homes. In addition, they spontaneously created informal rules that were patterned on community values of cooperation through honor and shame. Palestinian norms of doing business and conducting behavior in social, economic, and political spheres were encoded in these informal property rules inside the camps. In a transitional landscape where every aspect of a refugee's existence is threatened, this uniquely *Palestinian* set of rules is a powerful way of transmitting the community's identity in the face of outside threats. In the upcoming chapters I discuss the preservation of the community from state incorporation as new threats confronted Palestinian refugees in Jordan and Lebanon and how it becomes an important motivating theme in negotiations over formal property rights with outside political groups.

3

FORMAL PROPERTY RIGHTS IN REFUGEE CAMPS IN JORDAN

By the mid-1960s, Palestinians in Jordan had seemingly settled into a stable pattern of life inside the camps. Life moved beyond the basic struggle for survival, and a vibrant political economic life flourished. Moreover, as chapter 2 described, Palestinians had an informal set of rules based on strategically selected pre-1948 experiences that protected community assets and preserved a Palestinian way of life in the midst of chaos. However, the Arab defeat in the 1967 Arab-Israeli War, the influx of Gazan refugees, and the bloody battles of Black September decimated locally grown Palestinian institutions and reintroduced chaos inside Baqa'a, Wihdat, and Jerash refugee camps. Once again, Palestinians were pushed into conditions not of their choosing and forced to renegotiate the evolution of property rights.

In this chapter, I trace the formalization of property rights inside Palestinian refugee camps across Jordan. Using biographies and historical accounts of Jordanian leaders, I discuss the transformative events of the late 1960s with a focus on how regional and international battles destroyed the internal workings of Palestinian refugee camps. In the political vacuum following Black September in 1970, the Jordanian regime sought to quell Palestinian nationalism, tame the camps through co-optation of camp institutions, and enhance tax revenues from refugee businesses. Specifically, they compelled Palestinians to talk about the future of the camps in Jordanian-run camp services improvement committees (CSIC). Using interviews I learned that Palestinians, struggling to regain order in the midst of the chaos, were forced to negotiate the formalization of property rights. As the New Institutional Economics (NIE) perspective expected, Jordanian officials dominated the process and operated as the credible enforcer of formally defined titles. However, contrary to NIE arguments, Palestinians did not passively accept domination or remain "locked into" state efforts at incorporation. Instead, Palestinians strategically converted traditional ways of securing protection in chaos to fit with the new ruling political coalition inside the camps. In an imperfect manner, Palestinians created a parallel system of enforcing property ownership that melded informal Palestinian practices with Jordanian rules. The system permitted Palestinians to keep many political economic affairs within the community. Of course, they still confronted tension between Jordan's domination and the protection offered through formal property rights. Nevertheless, the resulting hybrid system of property rights demonstrates the resiliency of Palestinians in protecting their assets and community in the face of outside threats to the existing camp order.

SHOCKS TO THE EXISTING CAMP ORDER

In the late 1960s, a confluence of regional and international events created tragedy and chaos inside Baqa'a, Wihdat, and Jerash refugee camps. The camps were particularly vulnerable because of their transitional nature. They did not have a sovereign leader to defend or protect their interests on the global scale. As mentioned in chapter 1, the protection gap inside the camps was the result of Arab countries abstaining from the 1951 Convention that offered basic rights to refugees and assigned responsibilities to host states. Arab states did not want to remain responsible for the upkeep of Palestinian refugees. Because Palestinian refugee camps did not fall under the jurisdiction of the UNHCR, there was a purposeful legal protection gap. As a result, political forces outside their control often found a way of infiltrating and introducing chaos into the camps. In particular, the Arab defeat during the 1967 war, the influx of Gazans, and the battles of Black September altered the political landscape inside the camps. In the early years, Fatah played a salient role in camp life across Jordan. Though there were a variety of alternative political groups like the Popular Front for the Liberation of Palestine (PFLP), the Democratic Front for the Liberation of Palestine (DFLP), and Hamas vying for power and control, Fatah, a nationalist Palestinian group, played a critical role in crafting Palestinian institutions at the camp level (Brand 1988; Sayigh 1997). In the 1960s, Palestinian political identity manifested itself openly across camps in Jordan as Fatah unions, councils, and meetings flourished (Brand 1988; Sayigh 1997). But in 1965, Fatah began overstepping its political boundaries inside Jordan. At the 1965 Arab League meetings, the Palestine Liberation Organization (PLO) and King Hussein were openly hostile to one another.

Though Fatah was founded in 1959, it did not enjoy widespread popularity until after 1968. In particular, it was only *after* the old guard of the PLO and Arab countries endured the demoralizing 1967 defeat against Israel and Fatah won the battle of Karamah launched against Israelis in 1968 that it became a household name in Palestinian refugee camps (Sayigh 1997). The growth in Fatah's stature in the refugee camps was due to the "heroic image that guerrilla organizations gained as a result of the Karamah battle on March 21, 1968" (Shaul 1986). The battle involved a one-thousand-man Israeli raiding party and six hundred Palestinians supported by forty-eight Jordanian tanks, eleven artillery batteries, and two brigades of infantry (Shaul 1986, 13). The encounter ended with between 70 and 150 casualties and 130 prisoners among the Palestinians, and 23 dead, 70 injured, and 3 missing in action on the Israeli side (Shaul

1986, 13). Though Jordanians fought alongside Palestinians, the narrative of Jordanian participation is often obfuscated. Instead it was hailed as the first *Palestinian* military victory over the Israeli army since the war of 1948. After Karamah, "To declare Palestinian identity no longer means that one is a refugee or a second-class citizen. Rather, it is a declaration that arouses pride, because the Palestinian has become the *fida'i* or revolutionary who bears arms" (Sayigh 1997, 195). Yasser Arafat, a young revolutionary and a founding member of Fatah, capitalized on the guerrilla wins and pushed his grassroots political organization to capture a critical number of seats to control the fourth Palestinian National Council Meeting in Cairo in 1968. Arafat used this victory to nourish the self-esteem and image of Palestinians, to bolster the power of Fatah in comparison to other political groups competing for authority, and to oust the old guard of the PLO. In February 1969, Yasser Arafat and Fatah took control of the PLO.

In 1969, Fatah did not have international legitimacy as a representative of Palestinian refugees. It was a nascent political group, but its authority and legitimacy in representing the future of the Palestinian people was far from secure. Other Arab countries, like Jordan, and factions within the Palestinian political sphere were vying for control of the Palestinian national identity and representation on the international level. Fatah had to generate a Palestinian support base inside the camps.

At the same time, a large influx of Palestinian-Gazan refugees that had been living in Egypt poured into Jordan following the Arab defeat in 1967. In fact, Baqa'a and Jerash camps were built to handle the influx of Palestinians from Gaza. These refugees from Gaza, dispossessed for a second time, faced the same chaos that Palestinians had faced after the 1948 *Nakbah*. Fatah hoped to represent their plight in Jordan. In turn, Jordan felt that Gazans could disrupt the entire stability of the regime. It was a messy situation for Palestinians caught in the middle of elite politics.

Fueled by the destabilization of a new influx of Gazan refugees and the failure of Jordan in the 1967 Arab-Israeli War, Fatah initiated open attacks along the border with Israel (Sayigh 1997). Israeli counter- and preemptive attacks increased in number as well (Brand 1988, 169). For example, on June 3, 1970, Fatah launched a rocket attack on Beit Shean and Israel retaliated by bombing Irbid in Jordan, killing seven civilians, a solider, and injuring twenty-six others (Shlaim 2008, 318–19). The dangerous cycle of attacks launched by Fatah from refugee camp bases near Amman, Jordan, and counterattacks by Israel prompted increasing uneasiness in the Hashemite regime. The Jordanian military also felt humiliated by their inability to act against Israeli and Palestinian aggressions (Sayigh 1997, 192). In effect, Fatah threatened to undermine the Jordanian regime's long-term survival. The Hashemite monarchy, furious with Fatah's attacks and the difficult position it placed Jordan in with respect to the West, Israel, and its own military, engaged in several violent clashes with Fatah inside the refugee camps. In a biography of his life, Hussein later recalled,

> We had thousands of incidents of breaking the law, of attacking the people. It was a very unruly state of affairs in the country and I continued to try . . . towards the end I felt I was losing control. In the last six months leading up to the crisis the army began to rebel [against Fatah's behavior]. I think the gamble was probably the army would fracture along Palestinian-Jordanian lines. That never happened, thank God. (Shlaim 2008, 320)

By June 7, 1970, open fighting broke out between the Jordanian military and Fatah fighters in Zarqa refugee camp (Sayigh 1997). Two assassination attempts were made on King Hussein. In this context, the Bedouin units of the Jordanian military launched heavy shelling and fighting in Wihdat and Al-Husseini camps on the outskirts of Amman (Shlaim 2008, 320). After three days of fighting, a ceasefire was declared, but the deal was tenuous. Hussein's power was threatened and Palestinian authority seemed on the upswing inside Jordan. On August 15, 1970, Arafat reportedly said, "We have decided to convert Jordan in to a cemetery for all conspirators—Amman shall be the Hanoi of the revolution" (Shlaim 2008, 325). This set the stage for an all-out war between Palestinians and Jordanians. On September 17, 1970, King Hussein made the decision to "recapture his capital" and launched another attack (Sayigh 1997; Shlaim 2008, 327). After long and bloody battles on both sides, Fatah and other political groups were defeated and departed Amman to the northern part of Jordan in the 'Aljun hills, where they were finally expelled in July 1971 (Brand 1988; Sayigh 1997; Shlaim 2008). At a July 17, 1971, press conference, Hussein stated that Jordan was "completely quiet" and that there was "no problem" now (Shlaim 2008, 343). By July 1971, the final rupture between Jordan and the PLO was complete. King Hussein defeated Fatah-PLO forces and sought to establish Jordanian sovereignty in the camps and rebuild the Jordanian state. Locally contrived Palestinian political structures suffered "near-total destruction" and all Palestinian institutions, including informal property rights, were officially "closed" inside the camps (Brand 1988, 15, table 1.2, 171). In an interview, a Palestinian summarized how refugees felt following Black September. He succinctly noted, "We had now become a potential source of trouble. We knew we would face new levels of discrimination. The Gazan refugees would have it the worse because they were the newest" (I-3J). Another noted, "Again, we had to start from scratch in the camps and pull ourselves out of the dirt. We had done it before and we knew could do it again" (I-28J).

OUTSIDE DOMINATION OF PROPERTY RIGHT FORMALIZATION IN THE CAMPS

In this context, Jordan emerged as a powerful force in the political vacuum in the camps following Black September. Following the ouster of Fatah and other political groups, Jordan deeply entangled itself in refugee camp life. Jordanian entrance into the Palestinian refugee political fray was unprecedented. Legally, the refugee camps were purposefully devoid of a sovereign state due to the international legal quagmire of displacement and refugee status. Indeed, Jordan's abstention from the UNHCR's 1951 Convention with respect to caring for Palestinian refugees meant that Jordan did not have legal sovereignty in the camps, even though they asserted their authority following Black September.

Despite the legal oddity and messiness of Jordanian involvement in Palestinian refugee camps, the political ambiguity created an opportunity for institutional formalization. Jordanian authorities set up camp-level offices for the Department of Palestinian Affairs (DPA). The camp-level offices were known as the camp services improvement committees (CSIC). The CSIC housed Jordanian officials who were responsible for crafting formal property rights inside the camps among other things (www.dpa.gov.jo/). Consistent with the expectations of the New Institutional Economics approach, it was only after Jordanian intervention inside the camps' institutional structures that previously informal claims evolved into formal property rights. Jordan was a third-party enforcer that could credibly define formal property claims inside the camps.

Formal property rights in refugee camps like Baqa'a, Jerash, and Wihdat required refugees to legally register their property claims with the CSIC. The CSIC issued legal titles to assets in the camps (www.dpa.gov.jo/). The CSIC's system of registering existing claims to property mimicked how Jordanians registered property (I-2J, I-3J). Specifically, twenty-five out of twenty-eight business owners interviewed in Palestinian refugee camps in 2007 claimed that the system inside the camps was exactly like the system of property titles in Jordan. These were responses to distributional question number four in appendix B. Jordanian officials at the CSIC requested that refugees visit the local CSIC office and register their existing claims to resources so that formal titles could be issued (I-79J, www.dpa.gov/jo). Next, formal property rights permitted refugees to transfer property rights through the Jordanian officials located at the CSIC. Beginning in the early 1970s, the CSIC presided over basic property transactions in the camps like witnessing and writing contracts for camp residents (www.dpa.gov.jo/). The establishment of property rights ushered in police and security forces that monitored property inside the camps. The CSIC maintained the security and order of property by having police and civil defense stations throughout the camps. The DPA reports that there was one police station in Wihdat, one in Baqa'a, and one in Jerash. These police stations monitored criminal activity, including property violations. In addition to the police stations, the CSIC collected payments from businesses and residents to operate a local security force that patrolled property at night. The CSIC enforced property contracts by delivering suspected violators to the Jordanian judicial and penal system (I-71J).

In interviews, Palestinians described how they registered previously informal claims of ownership or rentals of homes and businesses inside the camps. An iron manufacturing business owner in Zarqa camp said, "My family has worked in iron welding for many years. I inherited this business from my father. For the last twenty-five years, I have formally owned it in my name. The government gives us the right to own a business or a home inside the camps. My title is registered at the CSIC" (I-21J). A glass manufacturing and design entrepreneur in Wihdat described the process of registering a previously informal property claim: "If I wanted to establish my ownership of the business, sell it, or rent the space then I was required to go to the CSIC to record my name or a buyer's name. We had to conduct this business in front of a witness and exchange payment there too" (I-85J). Another business owner reported, "The [Jordanian] government tightly regulates businesses in the camps. You must register the business and have an approved license. I don't own my place. I rent it from another refugee. I registered my rental in the CSIC" (I-16J). One refugee said, "I rent my spot in the camp from a family. I started many years ago paying about $700 U.S. dollars a month but now rent has gone up to $1500 U.S. dollars. I register my business at the CSIC" (I-17J). Many concluded, "There is a strong sense of law and order coming from Jordan. The security forces of the police and army patrol the main road frequently" (I-44J).

JORDANIAN ENGAGEMENT OF PALESTINIANS AT THE CSIC

After learning how Palestinians registered claims, the new system of formal property rights seemed entirely under the control of Jordanian authorities. From a theoretical standpoint, the process of formalization seemed to fit squarely with a New Institutional Economics perspective on institutional formalization. In keeping with the theory, Jordanian intervention was necessary to formalize titles.

Moreover, the structure of the CSIC reflected Jordanian domination of the camps. The DPA exerted almost complete control over the CSIC by setting the yearly budget for each refugee camp's CSIC office (I-1J, I-2J, I-3J; www.dpa.gov.jo/). In addition, the DPA selected CSIC members from the camp in coordination with the administrative governor of the area in which the camp is located (I-1J, I-2J, I-72J; www.dpa.gov/jo). Each camp had a centrally located CSIC office with roughly seven to thirteen Palestinian members representing various camp segments (I-1J, I-72J). It is important to note that the refugee camp members that serve on the CSIC did not represent different political parties because political groups are not encouraged in the camps (I-72J). This is an important difference between the functioning of local committees in Jordanian and Lebanese refugee camps. In Lebanon, Fatah set up local committees and different political interests were represented on the committee. The clusters of Palestinian refugees living in the camps also meant that Jordanian authorities could monitor and control their actions. "All refugee camps—even veritable townships like Aqabat Jabir, near Jericho, and Zarqa, near Amman—were closely guarded by armed forces, whether policy or army, that regulated refugees' communications with the outside world" (Dann 1989, 11).

Certainly, Jordanians had the power and means to impose an efficient system of formal property rights on the camps. Jordanian power over the camps was at its zenith after the decimation of Palestinian political institutions following Black September. Despite this power and potential for easy formalization and extractive revenue enhancement schemes, Jordanians painstakingly engaged Palestinians in negotiations, registration procedures, and enforcement strategies. Jordan engaged in talks with Palestinians through a series of ongoing micro-level dialogues at the CSIC.

CSIC offices were the local meeting spot for Palestinian sheiks and businessmen to negotiate the transition from informal claims to property to formal legal titles with Jordanians. These negotiations did not occur overnight, but were instead the result of a sustained dialogue between Jordanian officials and other members of the refugee community. Jordanians invited Palestinian refugee community leaders and businessmen to the CSIC to engage in a dialogue about the formalization of property rights.[1]

This was a clunky and costly process. Contrary to the expectations of New Institutional Economics, the new system of formal property rights was not very efficient. In fact, the process of formalization seemed inefficient by design. In interviews it was generally felt that "Jordanians and Palestinians cooperated and the CSIC acted as a meeting point for Jordanians and Palestinians. It was a place to share and exchange ideas about institutions, like property rights, inside the camps" (I-72J).

Why go to all the trouble of engaging with Palestinian refugees that had just caused a costly military battle if simple efficiency was the primary motivating force behind institutional formalization? Initially, after the devastation of Black September, Palestinians inside the camps feared that Jordanian involvement in camp affairs would prevent the ownership of businesses and homes in the camps like before their dominance. In particular, the Hashemite regime discouraged Palestinian aspirations. Jordan's dynastic territorial interests in the West Bank "clearly ran counter to aspirations for the recovery of all of Palestine followed by its establishment as an independent state. Political activities within Jordan were kept within the Hashemite framework" (Hamid 1975, 92).

Though Jordan said it would not push for institutions that enshrined a "Palestinian identity," they did hope to assimilate

Palestinians through a variety of political strategies, including the formalization of property rights that could meld a Jordanian and Palestinian identity. Sayigh notes, "Jordan sought actively to subsume the Palestinianism and to recast its Palestinian subjects as Jordanian citizens" (1997, 21). In an interview one respondent noted, "Jordan had a couple of goals during the formalization of titles inside the camps. First, the former minister of electricity noted that Jordanian officials realized the economic growth occurring in the camps and the tax revenue collection based on a system of formal titles helped them capture this wealth" (I-79J). Officials could capture the revenues of lucrative construction businesses through an efficient system of property titles (I-1J). More importantly, Jordan hoped to consolidate and "tame" the large Palestinian population through the registration and enforcement of property titles inside the camps. Indeed, the Hashemite regime strove to integrate the Palestinians into Jordanian society and argued that they were one indivisible people.

This motive for formalization is not surprising when one traces the behavior of King Hussein with respect to Palestinian identity and representation. For example, even in 1964 before Black September, Jordanians feared the rising power of the PLO, and King Hussein resisted early proposals made by the Arab League to create a Palestinian "entity." Hussein ultimately compromised whereby the United Arab Republic (UAR) and other Arab governments agreed that the Fatah-PLO would be institutionalized but it would not be permitted to challenge Jordan's sovereignty over West Jordan (Shlaim 2008, 206). Hussein wrongly assumed he could control the PLO by keeping it close by within the borders of Jordan, rather than far away hosted by another Arab country.

We know that the deal ultimately unraveled in Jordan in 1970, but it is clear from these early regional negotiations that Hussein insisted that Jordan *alone* officially spoke for the Palestinians within its borders. By 1969, the establishment of Fatah's authority in the PLO threatened to undermine the very foundations of the Hashemite Kingdom of Jordan that claimed to represent the

Palestinian population. This was reflected in a popular regime slogan, "Jordan is Palestine and Palestine is Jordan" (Shlaim 2008, 206). A carpenter in Irbid camp asserted, "The [Jordanian] government is in control of the camp's titling system here. Even still, I suppose things are pretty good for us. They are certainly better than in Lebanon and Syria" (I-46J).

Instead of excluding Palestinians from negotiations, Jordan pursued a political strategy of co-optation to placate and stabilize the refugee camps (Sayigh 1997). After Black September, it excluded only the most potent threats to their authority like the PLO-Fatah and other Palestinian political groups like the PFLP (Sayigh 1997). Though some Palestinians from the camp community were permitted to negotiate the new system of property rights at the CSIC, they faced a lot of difficulty in finding a Palestinian pathway for protection in the post–Black September political climate.

DYNAMIC RESPONSES TO JORDANIAN RULE

At the moment that Jordan asserted dominance in refugee camps, Palestinians were faced with a critical decision. During negotiations at the CSIC, they had to devise a strategy to avoid total state incorporation while still protecting assets. Palestinians could choose from a variety of strategic responses to Jordanian domination and forced formalization. I outline just a few to give an idea of the diverse trajectories Palestinians could have taken. First, Palestinians could have done nothing, remained passive, and fully submitted to Jordanian rule. Second, they could have forcefully rebelled against Jordanian rule and engaged in violent conflict to assert Palestinian independence. Finally, they could have pursued a middle path that balanced Palestinian desires for protection within the parameters of Jordanian rule.

At a critical juncture in the Palestinian narrative following the chaos of Black September, refugees did not passively accept Jordanian rule or violently clash with Jordanian forces again. Palestinians

did not get locked into their despair or pre–Black September informal property rights systems. In addition, they did not violently rebel
against Jordanian authority. These were wise strategic considerations because the first option would have destined the Palestinian
community to complete domination and co-optation by Jordanians.
The second path would have likely resulted in the loss of even the
most basic protections considering Fatah's recent defeat and King
Hussein's military might after Black September.

As Thelen suggests in her study of the evolution of vocational
institutions in Germany, individuals are constantly renegotiating
institutions on the ground (2004, 6). Palestinians wanted to work
within the new challenges they faced after Black September to create a system that melded Jordanian rules with their communal ideas
of how property should be protected. Palestinians strategically pursued a middle pathway. Palestinian members of the CSIC negotiated
a system of property rights that converted traditional Palestinian
ideas about property claim enforcement into a system that melded
with Jordanian rules.

Conversations with sheiks or community religious leaders and
business owners that were sitting members on the CSIC gave insight
into the Palestinian strategy during negotiations over property
rights formalization. Sheiks were respected older gentlemen that
represented the Palestinian community's position during property
rights negotiations at the CSIC. Sheiks were repositories of pre-
Nakbah (1948) Palestinian history and anchored the community's
beliefs and values in the context of the refugee camps (I-72J). Refugee sheiks hoped to give Palestinians a voice inside the CSIC during property rights negotiations (I-72J). They wanted a voice during
negotiations because they had just witnessed the failure of Fatah,
a group that had once served as the mouthpiece for the Palestinian community in Jordan. They hoped to balance Jordanian rules
with Palestinian desires for protection from state incorporation.
One sheikh said, "I hoped to incorporate Palestinian traditions of
justice into the shape and structure of the new property right system" (I-72J). Camp businesses that were present during negotiations

also wanted to increase the security of their assets *and* keep enforcement mechanisms within the Palestinian community in the new political economic climate. Many businesses were expanding and increasingly engaged in markets outside the camps in neighboring Jordanian towns and villages. "Having a title that recognized my ownership of a business by the Jordanians would give me greater security in our new situation. So naturally, we pushed for it [formal titles] to happen. But we wanted it to be done in a way consistent with Palestinian values" (I-20J).

Sheikhs and business owners of the CSIC had a deep reservoir of Palestinian institutional experiences from which to draw to guide the design of the new formal property rights system in Jordan. As outlined in chapter 2, they had a diverse set of Ottoman and British colonial experiences in land tenure rules. In addition, they had their post-*Nakbah* system of informal rules they could use as well. What parts of their group history would they strategically meld with Jordanian rules to protect the community and assets?

In interviews, I pressed Palestinians to expand on the process of formalization in the camps. I learned interesting responses when I asked sheikhs and business owners questions about safety and title enforcement practices inside the camps. "Do you feel safe in the camps? Do you feel your home or business is protected here? Why do you feel safe? Moreover, if you caught someone trying to steal or abuse your property (business/home), what would you do? Why do you resolve conflicts in this particular way?" The responses to these questions revealed a complex hybrid system of title enforcement in which Palestinians converted communal traditions of enforcement into the Jordanian-controlled system of formal property rights. An ironsmith in Baqa'a shared,

> Jordan wanted to control and formalize property rights. So we went along with some things they wanted—like for us to register claims at the CSIC. But inside the camps, it is really the Palestinian not Jordanian rules that win out. We have a Palestinian system of justice that runs parallel with, and sometimes intersects with the Jordanian one.

If things get too out of hand with family violence and revenge in the camps then we might go to the Jordanians but that is very rare. (I-4J)

Palestinians hoped to bring to bear templates of behavior that protected them in the past in similar situations. Specifically, Palestinians described how within the boundaries of the CSIC they converted their own ways of creating order using traditional values of family, honor, and shame from pre-*Nakbah* and pre–Black September experiences to meet the challenges of Jordanian domination and insulate the community. Though Jordanian courts were available to enforce claims and resolve disputes, Palestinians sought to keep problems within the camps. Refugees wanted to protect the community from Jordanian co-optation. They denied Jordanians full institutional access to the community by emphasizing old village and family traditions for resolving disputes.

The owner of a glass shop in Baqa'a explained how sheiks and business owners at negotiations insisted that enforcement remain at the local level instead of with the Jordanians. "Our religious and community values police the camps here. They are traditional values and rules that have always been around. And we use them here now. An outside force like the Jordanians did not do this for us" (I-12J).

In general, Palestinians felt very safe in Baqa'a, Wihdat, and Jerash camps because community and religious values anchored camp behavior even after the destruction of Black September. "Though we have a Jordanian court system and set of rules on the books, we tend to do it like Palestinians have always done. We deal with troubles in the family and in the community. The courts are available, of course. But they are costly in terms of my time and money" (I-43J). Moreover, "No one dares to do bad things because families rule in a close community like ours. If you behave badly then your entire family will suffer. It is like the olden days even now. I prefer to resolve disputes using family and village channels. The Jordanian courts are too costly for me" (I-6J). Another said, "I mostly rely on friends and family to resolve disputes and do business in the camps" (I-8J). A business owner in Wihdat camp gave insight into the complex system of enforcement in the camps: "I feel the area is very secure here for two reasons. In my opinion, people have good values. They have Palestinian values of honor and family responsibility. Second, the Jordanians have provided a strong sense of law and people naturally fear going to jail or sanctions" (I-41J).

In the camps, a unique system of title enforcement melded the Jordanian justice system and the Palestinian tribal, community, and religious systems to enforce titles. The Jordanian system of enforcement provided one level of protection: "There is a general sense of security here because of government control and protection of my business" (I-25J). But Palestinians were reluctant to use the Jordanian system as the first line of protection: "I rarely use the courts. In fact, I have only been once. I ultimately won but it was such a pain in the ass" (I-50J). In addition, "I feel the community is really secure here because of our values. I wouldn't go to the Jordanian courts because they are slow and very expensive. We can solve the problems right here without them" (I-29J).

Aside from frustrations with the lengthy process and fees associated with the courts, Palestinians avoided the courts to maintain their independence from the Jordanian state by resolving disputes within the confines of the camp community. One refugee said, "I prefer to not use the Jordanian courts to resolve conflicts. This is partly because the fees and time required are costly. But mostly, I want to keep this within the [Palestinian] community" (I-6J). Most Palestinians preferred to use traditional means of protection first. One refugee explained his thoughts on protection inside the refugee camps:

I live in a place where Allah, community, and self-policing are the first ways of protecting myself. If anything weird or strange occurs then it is usually seen by my neighbors. I don't like to rely on the courts. Instead, I use my friends and family to put pressure on anyone that might do something bad. If it is someone strange to me, from outside the camps, well then I might use the Jordanians to help me. (I-4J)

Interestingly, Palestinians understood they could not maintain complete independence from the state. To strike a balance between complete state incorporation and communal independence they adopted an enforcement system that permitted the Palestinian and Jordanian enforcement systems to intersect. Palestinians, like the Zomias responding to state encounters in Scott's (2009) *The Art of Not Being Governed*, merged their customs with those of their more powerful state neighbors in order to manage and repel complete state incorporation. Zomias had plastic notions of ethnic group identity that they deployed at key moments to assert common ground with and in some cases independence from more influential neighbors. For the Zomias it was a political strategy for survival to determine how much of their group's way of life should be melded with outsiders.

Indeed, Palestinians had a long history of negotiating their protection with powerful outsiders like the Ottoman Empire and British mandate authorities. Divine (1994) studies how everyday men and women in nineteenth- and twentieth-century Palestine managed their existence and protection in the face of outside rule. Though scholars commonly portray the Ottoman Empire as a blanket force that imposed authority and institution, their authority "did not come entirely at the expense of local autonomy and initiative" (Divine 1994, 2). Imperial infrastructure was not an "alien graft" on Palestinian communities because the "actions of ordinary people also shaped the way in which government institutions were structured and operated" (Divine 1994, 2–3). Institutions were created by pressures from within Palestinian societies that varied across villages and regions within the country. Though the Ottomans had a cohesive policy for the registration of *musha* or communal land use, for example, some communities were inclined to register their property with local religious courts while others operated informally without signed titles or contracts. The variation at the local level demonstrates how Palestinians engaged in what Divine calls "creative survival" (1994, 4). Just as Scott's (2009) analysis of the Zomias illustrates the plasticity of communal institutions, Divine similarly argues that Palestinians during the Ottoman era "changed their out-looks, their behaviors, and their relationships to make their way in increasingly changing circumstances" (1994, 4).

Palestinian refugees "creatively survived" institutional negoti-ations with Jordanians by reshaping traditional modes of protect-ing property and in turn avoided complete state incorporation. Palestinian customs of managing and enforcing property were not rigid rules incontrovertible to modern conditions. As a community living in a transitional space, Palestinians treated their traditions as "plastic" so they could meld and convert to the schemes of the new ruling coalitions. This was a political strategy for survival among Palestinian community members in Jordan. For example, the Jordanian and Palestinian enforcement systems worked in tan-dem to sanction title violators. A sheikh in Baqa'a camp revealed many of the intricacies of tribal law in the refugee camps in Jordan (I-72J). Jordanians allowed Palestinians to mete out a measure of enforcement and justice at the camp level because ultimately the Jordanian system set the boundaries for acceptable behavior. Pal-estinians agreed on this system because it gave them a measure of communal independence:

> Let me tell you how things happen here. For example, if an individual stole a piece of machinery from a carpentry business then the vic-tim would notify the head of his family of the problem. It is likely, because everyone is always watching and monitoring, that the busi-ness owner would have a suspect in mind or would hear through camp gossip the name of the culprit. Camp elders would gather to discuss the case and would bring the Holy Quran to swear on the facts of the case. The camp elders would bring the suspect and his family to ask for forgiveness from the victim's family and agree on a docu-ment of reconciliation. This was a binding document between fami-lies that would contain a specific amount of money [restitution] that was paid to the victim for the price of his machinery or damage to his business. All the relevant parties including village elders signed the document. (I-72J)

The sheik in Baqa'a revealed that

> Once the reconciliation document has been declared and signed
> then the matter might be closed. If it was very serious and the
> families were upset then we might take the letter to the CSIC and
> onto a local Jordanian judge where the state decided on how to
> deal with the guilty man. The judge could decide to incarcerate the
> man and rule that Jordanian officials could enter the camp with
> the help of the CSIC to extract the resident. The reconciliation
> document played a role in determining how the state would act.
> Sometimes the community guaranteed that they could control the
> guilty individual so the guilty man could avoid a jail sentence with
> the Jordanians. (I-72J)

The sheik's discussion demonstrates how Palestinians carved out a
sliver of Palestinian protection in a world of Jordanian domination.
Certainly refugees were still under the thumb of Jordanian rule, but
the dual enforcement system permitted Palestinians a middle pathway that balanced the need for protection and the reality of Jordanian dominance. Though it was not a perfect system, Palestinians
avoided worse alternatives like total state incorporation and communal destruction. In summary, Palestinians responded to shifting conditions in the transitional camp landscape. Past traditions
of managing property did not remain frozen in time. Accordingly,
Palestinians converted their traditional community experiences in
managing property rights to work with the newly imposed parameters of Jordanian control inside the camps.

THE TENSION IN PROTECTION AND PREDATION

Refugees felt that the dual systems worked well together, though
imperfectly. Indeed, a central theme I heard from refugees during
my study of institutional evolution among transitional communities was the tradeoff between institutionalized protection and
institutionalized predation. During interviews, respondents were

conflicted in their representation of Jordanian authority and the nature of protection in the camps.

On one hand, refugees felt the Jordanian system guaranteed legal protection: "I have been in business for twenty-five years here. I think nowadays people feel this place is generally secure because of the police, guards, and rule of law" (I-35J). Others were careful to attribute their protection to a combination of community values and Jordanian law. For example, one refugee said, "I feel protection because of people's values *and* the strength of law" (I-21J). On the other hand, upon deeper reflection, some were not so sure that the Jordanians had good intentions in using the law or security forces to protect Palestinians. Instead Jordanians were characterized as more interested in protecting their own people from Palestinians. An iron welder said, "Yes, it is safe here. We have our way of life and community values make us feel safe. People have respect for the Jordanians. . . . *Well.* . . . No, no that is not true. I think we *mostly fear* the Jordanians and the police" (I-60J).

During interviews refugees expressed an underlying sense that Jordanians assisted in protection but that their presence also exposed Palestinians to predation. The tension between submitting to Jordanian domination while carving a small sliver of Palestinian order created vulnerabilities to the community. Palestinians learned that by institutionalizing Jordanian forms of protection they were potentially institutionalizing Jordanian predation of their own politically weaker community as well.

This issue of institutionalized predation was evident among certain portions of the Palestinian community. Palestinian refugees from the Gazan conflict felt especially vulnerable to Jordanian predation because they lacked any special status in Jordan: "Those Palestinians from Gaza [1967] that are without *wasta* [political connection or corruption] do not always do well here" (I-42J).

This vulnerability to predation was clearest in Jerash refugee camp. The majority of the camp population had Palestinian Gazan refugee status. Palestinians from Gaza lacked any citizenship claims in Jordan. With the exception of a few families who had political connections and were able to obtain citizenship through royal decrees, most Palestinians from Gaza were treated as refugees with only partial benefits and sought shelter in one of the six emergency camps set up in the wake of the 1967 war. These refugees hold temporary passports and must have a local Jordanian partner or receive the approval of a ministerial council to own property outside the refugee camps. Compared to Wihdat and Baqa'a, Jerash camp contained the highest concentration of Palestinian refugees that came from Gaza and held limited benefits in Jordan. The chart, gleaned from el-Abed (2005) in chapter 1, highlights disparities in refugee status in Jordan. A refugee carpenter with Gazan status in Jerash camp explained his situation:

> I registered my place with the CSIC, originally I bought the place from another Palestinian family that was able to leave the camp shortly after we got here. The CSIC completely controls titling. When I confront a problem with stealing, I try to use tribal law. Of course, there are issues. Sometimes, I can't resolve the problem with family, especially when I do business with people from outside the camp. I will try to use the Jordanian courts but there is a problem. I am a Gazan and I have no *wasta* [political connection]. Things are slower and costly for me. I believe they are worse for me than other Palestinians because I am from Gaza. (I-91J)

He felt that the CSIC and camps with more refugees from Gaza were under greater Jordanian control and scrutiny than Wihdat and Baqa'a camps. In his opinion, those other camps fared better because they had fewer percentages of Palestinians from Gaza in their population. "In my opinion, the CSIC is mostly an agent of the government *mukhabarat* [secret police]. They collect information about us to make sure we behave properly. Being a Gazan in Jordan makes life harder than if I were just a regular Palestinian here" (I-91J). Another carpenter in Jerash reiterated the challenging situation for the Gazans: "I try to use tribal law and Palestinian ways of doing business. But the *mukhabarat* and the government are ever present. They are a hindrance to us. We must register all activity with the CSIC and they control it. They don't want us to organize ourselves alone" (I-96J). An aluminum business owner said that for enforcement, "The focus is usually on tribal law and family, for me. But the government is a pain. It [the Jordanian government] treats us as a security threat and interferes with our way of life" (I-95J).

Residents in Wihdat and Baqa'a did not emphasize the *mukhabarat* or secret police in interviews. I am fairly certain the *mukhabarat* are ever present in camps across Jordan, but communities with higher numbers of 1948 Palestinians did not emphasize or mention their presence to me. Moreover, they were less likely to see the government as a "hindrance" and more as a "helpful" resource when it came to enforcement involvement in the camps. In Jerash camp, an iron welder said, "In day-to-day life, tribal law is the best thing to rely on because I feel the government is mostly a hindrance here. They say they provide 'security' here for us. But is the security for us or for them?" (I-90J). This tension, though markedly more evident in Jerash camp, was not entirely absent in other camps. For example, in Wihdat camp one person said, "The area is very secure here. People have good values. Problems are very rare. But we all fear getting involved with the Jordanians. Going to jail there is very bad for us Palestinians" (I-41J). Another Wihdat resident said, "I guess I feel safe here. The Jordanian patrols here are an ever-present threat here. They make me feel secure living on this main street but they also scare me too. You know?" (I-33J).

Jordanian enforcement mechanisms like police patrols, prison sentences, and tough fines enhanced the safety of assets, but also made Palestinians feel that they were constantly monitored and vulnerable to Hashemite power. Property rights were supposed to offer Palestinians protection from chaos, but the system negotiated with Jordanians also left them open to predation. The case of Palestinians formalizing property rights in Jordan after Black September shows that communities in transitional settings face challenging constraints for finding protection in the midst of chaos and more powerful neighbors that seek to control power and resources on the ground. In the face of these parameters, Palestinians searched for what Qian (2003) calls the "feasible" pathway to protection that balanced protection with outside domination. Transitional communities rarely have the opportunity to create "best practice" forms of institutions (Qian 2003). As a result, the pursuit of protection through property rights in imperfect transitional conditions unintentionally opened the community up to predation.

This chapter traced the formalization of property rights in Jordan following the tumultuous events of the Arab-Israeli War and Black September. Jordan pursued a strategy of title formalization to reap the revenues of vibrant camp businesses and to co-opt Palestinian politics. Under the domination of the CSIC, Palestinians melded their own institutions with Jordanian rules. In particular, they converted their previous experiences in enforcement based on shared tribal and community patterns of life into a system that worked in tandem with the Jordanian judicial system. Though this offered a measure of order in the political wilderness of camp life, it also exposed them to Jordanian predation. This tension was most evident in places like Jerash refugee camp where Gazans without legal status were more highly concentrated. Despite its shortcomings, the system of formal property rights in refugee camps across Jordan reflects the tenacity and resilience of Palestinians working to find protection in a transitional space.

4

FORMAL PROPERTY RIGHTS IN REFUGEE CAMPS IN LEBANON

The abrupt departure of Fatah, a nascent Palestinian political group, from Jordan and its emergence as a formidable political power in refugee camps in Lebanon in 1969 and 1970 caused a shift in the ruling coalition inside Nahr al-Bared, Beddawi, al-Buss, and Rashidieh refugee camps. Similar to the chaos after Black September in Jordan, the new political leadership in camps across Lebanon shook-up life and created another critical moment for Palestinians to renegotiate property rights (I-1L).

In this chapter, I trace the formalization of property rights in Palestinian refugee camps in Lebanon. Following the signing of the Cairo Accords in 1969, Fatah established sovereignty in the refugee camps and set out to co-opt and control political economic life there. In particular, they set up camp committee (CC) offices to renegotiate property right claims. Using historical accounts and personal interviews with Fatah members, Fatah expressed a desire to represent Palestinian identity and nationalism in the camps. One way to go about its "revolutionary agenda" and engage in proto-state building was to craft formal property rights.

In response to Fatah's agenda, Palestinian refugees said they hoped to protect their assets from predation and to express their communal identity in the new parameters of Fatah rule. After a series of ongoing conversations at CC offices, Fatah and community members created a system of formal property rights in private and shared asset sectors. Consistent with New Institutional Economics (NIE), Fatah's intervention in camp affairs inspired formalization of previously informal property rights claims. Fatah served as a third-party enforcer. However, the system was limited in the consistency of enforcement across sectors. Specifically, the abuse of shared resource sectors like electricity and water exposed the tension between protection and predation that Fatah introduced into camp life.

1969: A NEW (DIS)ORDER IN PALESTINIAN REFUGEE CAMPS IN LEBANON

In 1969 and 1970, Fatah overstepped political boundaries inside Jordan. Fatah departed Jordan following a bloody battle known as Black September. By 1970, most Palestinian political institutions were destroyed in Jordan (Brand 1988, 15, table 1.2; Sayigh 1997, 192). After Fatah's departure from Jordan, the party set about establishing power in Lebanon. Fatah took advantage of fractures in the Lebanese political landscape and signed the 1969 Cairo Accords (Sayigh 1997). A Lebanese Maronite official described the difficult position Lebanon faced at the time: "The Lebanese 'state' was faced with two evils, a destructive civil war or this accord, which it was [thus] compelled to accept" (Sayigh 1997, 194). The agreement gave Fatah authority inside refugee camps in Lebanon (Rubenberg 1983; Sayigh 1997).

Palestinians in camps across Lebanon had mixed emotions about Fatah's newfound power in the camps. On one hand, the arrival of an outsider, albeit a Palestinian one, overturned the operation of established informal norms of doing business and owning property. A tile and concrete block manufacturer in Nahr al-Bared described how he felt about the critical moment of Fatah's arrival in 1969:

> I started in this industry by working for a Lebanese concrete block press factory as a laborer. It was back-breaking work. But after a while, I saved nine hundred Lebanese pounds, which was about $275.00. I bought myself a manual mold and started my own business in Nahr al-Bared. In the early years my business was just run on community rules, there were no set codes. Everything changed in 1969 when Abu Ammar [the local familiar name for Yasser Arafat] arrived. He came to shake everything up. We had a new group to contend with now. 1969 was a critical moment. (I-1L)

On the other hand, many Palestinians were excited to finally have a powerful group that purportedly represented Palestinian nationalism and championed the cause of the everyday Palestinian refugee. Until that point, Palestinian refugees felt they lacked a voice in international affairs. Unlike the older generation of Palestinian leaders, Arafat's Fatah intentionally focused on cultivating the Palestinian identity in the refugee camps. For example, in an interview one refugee expressed the hope that Fatah offered: "Before Fatah arrived, there was no one we could trust to express our Palestinian identity in the world. When Fatah arrived, we felt they represented a revolution. The world would take Palestinian refugees seriously" (I-33L).

A brief historical discussion of Fatah's political model is important for understanding why some Palestinians felt excited about their arrival. Fatah's political model represented a drastic departure from traditional Arab politics. In 1958, Yasser Arafat and two close friends, Abu Iyad and Faruq Qaddumi, became active Palestinian organizers in Kuwait (Rubin 1994, 7). Their level of political activism grew, and by the following year they founded *Filastinuna (Our Palestine)*, newspaper in Beirut. In October 1959, along with another friend named Abu Jihad, the crew of young Palestinian activists officially founded their own Palestinian nationalist group called *Fatah*. In Arabic, Fatah stands for *Harakat al-Tahrir al-Filastiniyya* (Palestine Liberation Movement), whose acronym reversed spells "Fatah," which means "conquest" (Rubin 1994, 7). While Arafat and his group of close friends worked to organize Fatah, other Arab states like Jordan and Egypt engaged in an interstate competition over representation of the Palestinian question in the international arena. Unlike Fatah, which represented a grassroots method of political and military organization, Arab states sought to impose a structure of Palestinian leadership from above. As a result, the Palestine Liberation Organization (PLO) was created in 1964 by Arab states at the Arab Summit meeting. Ahmad al-Shuqayri, selected as the Palestinian delegate to the Arab League by the Palestine National Council at a meeting in East Jerusalem, was also selected as the first chairman of the PLO by other Arab states (Rubin 1994, 8). Notably, the voices of everyday Palestinians were absent during the election of Shuqayri. He represented a traditional-style Arab political leader that the new generation of Palestinians felt had failed to accurately represent and defend the Palestinian position in domestic, regional, and international political arenas. In fact, "Far from creating effective popular control, he [Shuqayri] raises a possibility of return to the wretched manner in the Arab Higher Council Committee conducted the struggle of the Palestinian people before the disaster [of 1948]" (Shaul 1986, 3–4).

A schism between the PLO and Fatah developed early on. At the core, the two organizations represented divergent views on the level of Palestinian activism necessary for the shared goal of realizing Palestinian statehood. On one hand, Shuqayri and the PLO felt Arab states would defeat Israel without Palestinian guerilla actions. In contrast, Arafat's Fatah would win the mandate of the Palestinian people through local-level political and military organization. In effect, guerilla action would be necessary (Rubin 1994, 8). The swift and embarrassing Arab defeat during the 1967 war against Israel encouraged Arafat and Fatah more generally to push for a locally grown type of Palestinian activism in order to realize their political goals. Fatah openly criticized Shuqayri's participation in the 1967 Arab-Israeli War and pushed for a change in the leadership of the Palestinian people in the PLO. Moreover, Arafat focused his attention in the refugee camps teeming with "disinherited" Palestinian refugees (Sayigh 1997, 239). Fatah hoped to generate a Palestinian refugee support base in Lebanon, and leveraging formal property rights was one way to do this.

Though the Sugden's spontaneous order approach would expect property rights to emerge organically, the NIE perspective emphasizes the importance of a powerful political group, like Fatah, to trigger the formalization of property rights (Hajj 2014). Notably, NIE scholars might contend that Fatah was motivated to create a formal titling system to reap the economic benefits of increased tax revenues that are part and parcel of titling. However, in this case, findings departed from the NIE because Fatah did not expect the titling system or a system of taxes to bring in revenue. Indeed, Sayigh notes that the PLO-Fatah was less interested in extracting revenue from Palestinian refugees and more inclined to cultivate and co-opt Palestinian society through its own institutions (1997, iix–ix). He describes the political framework as a corporatist structure whereby the PLO-Fatah acted as the center of the political sphere and other political groups were subsumed by its institutions. Interestingly, Fatah's main source of revenue came from other Arab states. In fact, Arafat was aware of the importance of courting Arab states for Fatah's funding. Often, Fatah's political preferences would clash with the ideological interests of Arab states. Yet Arafat and the PLO-Fatah understood that outside funding was critical to their organizational success. Fatah did not look to the refugee camps for revenue. In a January 23, 1969, interview with *al-Sayyad* (Beirut), Arafat lamented provocatively,

I am a refugee. . . . Do you know what it means to be a refugee? . . . I have nothing, for I was banished and dispossessed of my homeland. . . . I want the homeland even if the devil is the one to liberate it for me. Am I in a position to reject the participation or assistance of any man? Can I be asked, for example, to refuse the financial aid of Saudi Arabia with the claim that it belongs to the [ideological] right?[1] After all, it is with the Saudi's money that I buy arms from China. (Shaul 1986, 38)

Arafat clearly outlined Fatah's dependence on outside assistance for revenue enhancement even if it meant "dealing with the devil." Interview evidence indicates that titling revenue would primarily pay for the functioning of the titling system. For example, a CC member said that "the fees associated with creating a formal title barely covered the cost of a notary, paper, photocopier, and record maintenance" (I-48L). Revenue enhancement schemes were not the main motivating force for Fatah to push for the formalization of property rights in Palestinian refugee camps in Lebanon.

Instead Fatah leveraged formal property rights to garner a loyal following in the camps (Sayigh 1997). This finding clearly departs from existing NIE arguments that maintain formal property rights are primarily motivated by economic efficiency and profit maximization. Using formal property rights, Fatah hoped to capitalize on Palestinian alienation and thirst for belonging to garner a following. In Fawaz Turki's memoir *The Disinherited*, the sense of alienation and isolation from Lebanese and fellow Arabs is eloquently described:

> Living in Beirut as a stateless person . . . I did not feel I was living among "my Arab brothers." I did not feel I was an Arab, a Lebanese, or as some wretchedly pious writers claimed, a "Southern Syrian." I was a Palestinian. And that meant I was an outsider, an alien, a refugee and a burden. To be that, for us, for my generation of Palestinians, meant to look inward, to draw closer, to be part of a minority that had its own way of doing and seeing and feeling and reacting. (Turki 1972, 8)

Turki indicates the internal longing that many Palestinians had for a broader national movement that represented their interests. Turki further describes how Palestinians could not look to other Arabs for help in this endeavor: "We were discriminated against on every level in Arab society. . . . Socially, Palestinians were despised, persecuted, or at least ignored. . . . I hated first the Arabs, then, in an inarticulate and vague manner, the world" (Turki 1972, 40).

Following the Arab defeat in 1967, Edward Said reflected on what the humiliating defeat meant for Palestinian national identity. "For the first time, after 1967 it became possible not only to become Palestinian again but to choose Fatah, or the Popular Front, or the Democratic Front as one's movement of choice: each was Palestinian, jealously guarding its own vision of a Palestinian future" (Said 1994, xv). Arafat, using his authority in Fatah and the PLO, was poised to fill this political vacuum for "disinherited" Palestinian refugees in Lebanon. He answered the call of Turki and many other refugees like Said. He wore the black-and-white-checkered *kaffiya*, a traditional Palestinian headscarf that identified him as an everyday Palestinian (Sayigh 1997) and proclaimed, "Our new [Palestinian] generation is tired of waiting for something to happen. Isn't it better to die bringing down your enemy than to await a slow, miserable death rotting in a tent in the desert?" (Rubin 1994, 19).

Arafat aimed to protect Fatah's role as the sole legitimate representative of the Palestinians throughout their diaspora (Shiblak 1997). In an illuminating interview with me, a Fatah party member commented that it was "only natural for Fatah to lead the formalization of property rights because Fatah was *umm al thawra* or 'The Mother of the [Palestinian] Revolution'" (I-48L).

This revolutionary slogan was constantly repeated in interviews with Fatah and everyday residents to emphasize the strength and authority of Fatah inside the camps. It is not my intention to suggest that Fatah was the *only* political group in the refugee camps. Certainly, Fatah played a dominant role in the PLO and in various refugee camps, but it was not the only party, nor did it have the same strength over the course of the past fifty years. Power waxed and waned in Lebanon depending on broader regional and international entanglements. It had to contend with various parties like the PFLP, DFLP, and Hamas. Despite their shifting power over time, Fatah played a critical role in establishing the basic structure of the formal property rights systems through the CC offices that persist until today across camps in Lebanon, with the exception of NBC after the 2007 conflict. "We were The Mother of the Revolution and we promised to care for Palestinians. We gave money to poor families, families of martyrs, widows, and orphans" (I-95L). Another said,

"We wanted to provide dignity and hope for Palestinians and to give them voice" (I-55L). Posters of Arafat, Fatah's main political figurehead, exclaiming, *"YOU [Arafat] INSPIRED IN US . . . A REVOLUTION!"* paper camp pathways even today. A poster from a 2012 research trip in Beddawi camp visually supports this claim (see figure 4.1).

FIGURE 4.1 Arafat political poster in 2012.

FATAH'S CAMP COMMITTEE OFFICES

During surveys and interviews, Fatah members also expressed their hope to consolidate popular authority through the mechanical aspects of a formal titling system (I-4L, I-23L, I-33L, I-34L, I-48L, I-54L, I-55L). Fatah hoped that the formal titling system would help them cultivate popular support because it increased interactions between Fatah officials and camp residents. To meet these goals, Fatah established camp committee (CC) offices and invited an array of local political and economic groups to participate in ongoing discussions over the new system of property rights at CC offices. To afford the CC infrastructure, Fatah cultivated and courted funding from Arab states like Iraq, Egypt, and Syria. Using this funding, Fatah set up a network of economic enterprises employing three thousand people in the camps, established hospitals, built orphanages, erected schools, and engaged in the development of a working police and judicial system (Rubin 1994, 44; Sayigh 1997, 239). Specifically, financial resources from other Arab states assisted in the setup of CC offices. Even though Fatah officials led the committees, the membership and structure of the committee configured to the local politics inside each camp (I-33L, I-34L, I-48L, I-54L, I-55L, I-58L, I-80L).

In a study of Nahr al-Bared's governance structure, Hanafi and Long identify the prominence of Fatah-PLO leadership in the camps in the 1970s and 1980s. Though other groups competed for power, Fatah controlled camp institutions (Hanafi and Long 2010, 31). Across camps and over time, CC offices resembled slight variations on a similar theme. New political groups entered the political fray, especially following the Lebanese civil war in 1982, but these new groups were incorporated into the existing CC member structure. Variations in the membership and size of the committees reflected differences in the local camp political landscape. "The CCs were created to deal exclusively with the issues of the Palestinian refugee. Each camp has their own office" (I-25L).

For example, Beddawi was a relatively small camp compared to NBC with a unique constellation of political groups that reflected local dynamics (I-33L, I-34L, I-48L, I-54L, I-55L, I-58L, I-80L). Beddawi had twenty-three committee members. These twenty-three members represented different interests: one head committee member (Fatah), sixteen Palestinian groups represented, four representatives, one from each different geographical "district" inside the camps, one UNRWA representative, and one religious figure. Each political group was granted the same number of representatives that were elected by party members, whereas "district" representatives reflected the popular vote of camp residents from the district and could come from any political party or union. There was not a regular reelection schedule. Once a representative was tired of the job or the community was discontented, a new election would be held (I-58L). The committee also permitted attendance but not CC membership to workers' unions and professional associations in the camps.

In contrast, NBC's CC had thirty-four members. Membership was broken down according to the following structure: sixteen political parties with equal membership, one committee leader, five geographic "districts" with five popularly elected members, two women's representatives, three trade union members, two engineering association members, two members from the teaching union, two from the doctor's union, and one religious official. The unions were official members and carried more weight in NBC politics than in Beddawi. The camp also had an additional district because of the larger size of the camp population. On the eve of property rights formalization in refugee camps in Lebanon, Fatah claimed that the CC offices were "the Palestinian people" or the "institutional expression" of their nation and their nationalist movement (Rubenberg 1983).

Initially, it seemed strange that Fatah invited a variety of political parties and business groups to property rights negotiations when it had the power to expropriate resources on its own or formalize property rights without community involvement. In effect, Fatah could have imposed an efficient system on the camps or simply expropriated resources for its own benefit without community consultation. After deeper consideration, the integration of a variety of groups into titling negotiations served as further evidence of Fatah's desire to control, co-opt, and nurture a base of political support in the camps. Camps in Lebanon are marked by many layers of community actors vying for power and control, like the Popular Committee lead by Fatah, the Armed Struggle Group, the Security Committee, smaller political factions, camp notables, various professional unions, and NGOs (Hanafi and Knudsen 2010a, 34). Integrating different groups into title negotiations "has been a conscious policy of Fatah in an attempt to co-opt the commando groups and moderate their behavior through participation in the civil institutions" (Rubenberg 1983, 12).

Some note that Fatah pursued a "dual policy" in the camps to cultivate and co-opt a following. For example, Fatah staffed PLO departments with its own members. This was particular true in departments like the "Martyr Fund" and the "Red Crescent Society" (Sayigh 1997, 239). On the other hand, it expanded PLO institutions at the camp level and offered posts at all levels, especially in the camp committees, to other guerilla groups according to a fixed quota. "To reinforce cooptation and widen its constituency still further, Fatah supported the expansion of committees in order to offer seats to smaller groups and bring them into the PLO framework" (Sayigh 1997, 239). It was a corporatist framework that sought to include many factions within the camps. Interestingly, the principle rival guerrilla groups in the refugee camps were happy to operate by the PLO-Fatah rules because it gave them and their constituency a guaranteed voice in camp affairs (Sayigh 1997, 239).

In sum, Fatah strategically used the *umm al thawra* slogan during negotiations to co-opt and garner a loyal following, even from oppositional political parties. Arafat announced that "Fatah will be the leader and the Palestinian people the vanguard" of the Palestinian state-building endeavor (Rubin 1994, 23). Fatah set up negotiations for formal property rights to co-opt and control the refugee camps. It hoped to institute changes in the camps from the ground up through the local camp committee offices.

PALESTINIAN REFUGEES NEGOTIATE
TITLE FORMALIZATION

After Fatah established authority through the Cairo Accords in 1969 and built CC offices, Palestinian communities were pushed to negotiate the formalization of property rights with Fatah's new ruling coalition. The CC offices were local gathering spots for the negotiation of formal property rights. Negotiations were an ongoing process involving a series of accumulated micro-level encounters between Fatah and different refugee community members like business associations, unions, and smaller political parties. Interestingly, though Fatah was dominant in the CCs, it limited or shackled its own power to expropriate title contracts through a voting system that gave each local political party a voice on issues of dispute. CC members consulted with one another and voted in the event of a property title dispute. Decisions were based on simple majority votes, though the CC sought consultative compromise on every issue (I-58L). In effect, the CC voting system served as a form of checks and balances that limited the power of Fatah and enforced contracts for all members of the camps, not just some members. Refugees from the camps had different perspectives on Fatah and inclinations about how to preserve assets and protect the community from predation. On one hand, many businesses and everyday residents were excited about Fatah and its revolutionary agenda. On the other hand, religious sheiks felt it was important to insulate the community's affairs from Fatah's elite politics in order to protect the community.

For example, refugee businesses had a big stake in the formalization of property rights. Once CCs were set up, businesses finally had a meeting place to talk about their needs regarding the protection of their assets. These small business entrepreneurs had more invested inside the camps than most residents and would see the most returns on investments with the construction of a formal property rights system that protected their assets. For example, businesses in the refugee camps in Lebanon had an average of four full-time workers and mostly conducted business inside the refugee camps or in nearby villages (from questions A2 and A3 on the background of construction businesses in appendix B). A number of businesses attended property rights negotiations at CC offices, including businesses in the carpentry, iron, steel, tile, cement, and glass-making subsectors.

In order to assess the motives of refugee businessmen, I primarily relied on survey data conducted in 2007 and in-depth interview data collected in 2004. Three questions in the survey focused specifically on the goals of businessmen as they sought to craft property rights. First, I asked businessmen if they primarily wanted to create property rights that facilitated long-distance business transactions. Indeed, most refugees wanted property rights that would facilitate long-distance transactions. Second, I asked businessmen if they desired rules that made it easier to do business with not only friends or family, but also with strangers. Not surprisingly, refugees wanted to overcome the challenges of refugee camp isolation. They desired a system that let them connect to individuals and companies outside the camps. Finally, refugee businessmen were asked if they wanted to create rules that worked primarily to enhance the success and efficiency of their business. Again businessmen predictably hoped to create efficient property rights.

While this data gave a general idea of their goals, in-depth interviews conducted in 2004 gave greater insight into the high transaction costs businessmen faced and how they sought to remedy the situation with a system of formal property rights. Most Palestinian refugee businessmen suffered from information asymmetries inside Lebanon because of the political, social, and economic isolation of the camps. Refugees had little information regarding the market value of their assets inside and outside the refugee camps. The information refugees could access was usually the result of personal experiences in factories or shops where they once worked. For example, a carpentry business owner named Ahmad said that he learned the craft of carpentry, the price of products in Beirut and Tripoli markets, and the value of carpentry assets through jobs he held in woodworking shops in Beirut (I-15L).

If businessmen did not have personal experiences like Ahmad, there was no systematic database where they could research the value of their assets. As a result of this information asymmetry, many businessmen in the camps sought a formal database of property titles broken down by residential vs. commercial business sector, the estimated value of the title, and a history of the property. Formal property rights would help overcome many of the problems they faced inside the camps.

Aside from business interests in pushing for formalization, residents expressed a high level of fear and uncertainty of their treatment outside the camps. Palestinians even felt unprotected on minor issues of safety like keeping a road functional for traffic. For example, a resident noted, "When I asked if they [the Lebanese officials] would fix the main road running through the camp, the official said to me, 'fix it yourself or don't. It is your problem. Go plant potatoes on it and make it a farm, for all I care'" (I-9L). Another refugee explained, "We have no legality outside the camps but we wanted legal protection inside the camps" (I-18L). Some residents looked to Fatah to fill the protection gap. A resident summarized their feelings about formalization: "Formal titles would keep us safe and Fatah said they could do it" (I-17L).

Unlike the attitude of fear and weariness among refugees toward Jordanian authorities, many Palestinians in Lebanon were excited to welcome Fatah's involvement in camp affairs. Camp residents negotiated titles because it met their desire for protection of a communal identity, especially because Fatah was willing to merge its own political desires with existing Palestinian norms of doing business. "We trusted them [Fatah] to make positive changes. After all, they said they would bring the revolution. We wanted to work with them to protect our interests in these changes" (I-34L).

Alternatively, some Palestinian community members like sheikhs (religious leaders) and family elders looked at the CC negotiations as a critical opportunity for protecting assets and communal identity. In particular, they hoped to integrate informal norms of doing business into the new formal system to insulate the community from

Fatah's elite politics. One interviewee said, "Before the CCs there was no way to legally own or claim a business. Before, we used to just use two men and the Quran to witness a title. Now with the CC, we have the chance to make it official but it is important to keep our traditions alive" (I-37L). Also another said,

> I still have my papers and keys to my farm in Palestine. But life here is now much more complex and we want to protect ourselves here in Lebanon so we are going to need papers too so we work with Fatah. Fatah could take what we were already doing and make it official. Still, we needed to preserve our way of doing things too, not just the way Fatah wants it. (I-39L)

THE STRUCTURE OF FORMAL PROPERTY RIGHTS IN THE CAMPS ACROSS LEBANON

Fatah's desire to consolidate power, the push for asset protection among camp businesses, and the desire of everyday residents to protect their community from full co-optation by Fatah were overlapping and mutually reinforcing incentives that prompted a strategic alliance conducive to formalization of property rights.

The resulting system created a dual structure for registering and enforcing an individual's informal claim to an asset. It melded Fatah's formal procedures with refugees' informal norms of resolving disputes through community consensus. The titles in appendix A reflect the templates for property rights ownership used in camps across Lebanon.

> With the help of Fatah, we created a system to make contracts. At the CC we could make a contract, including ones for sales and rentals, and they would witness the agreements. We paid a small fee of $17–25 U.S. dollars to make the agreement, make copies, and store duplicates in the CC offices. To register an informal claim, we bring outside papers from UNRWA if we have the. The camp committee

doesn't require this if the claim is "known" to be owned by the families making the agreement. Our copies of the files are kept in locked cabinets in the CC offices. Any disputes we might have are resolved by committee members voting on this issue, they work for consensus. (I-34L)

The CC enforced titles and resolved property disputes based on legal precedent. In one instance, I had the opportunity to witness a present-day case that was brought to the CC for adjudication (I-55L). The procedures for resolving disputes have largely stayed the same since the CC first formed. A woman came into Beddawi's CC visibly upset about the sale of the roof of her home. The woman was a widow who lived in the house with her young daughters. Her husband's brother owned the title to the home because the property was left to him for inheritance purposes. The husband's brother needed extra money and decided to sell the roof of the woman's home to a young man so that he could build another level onto the house. In effect, the home would become an apartment building. The woman objected to the sale of her roof because she did not know the family of the young man that bought the roof and she questioned his honorability. She worried that the young man would attack her daughters when she was not there to supervise the home.

The CC used cellphones to call several members of the committee to decide on the matter. CC members consulted with one another, referred to Islamic law, discussed previous cases that were similar, and took a simple majority vote. At the outset, the CC made it clear in front of all the transacting parties that the brother-in-law could sell the property without consultation of the widow *but* they hoped a compromise could be reached. Importantly, all parties (CC members, brother-in-law, widow) remembered that the Quran asks all Muslim communities to protect those segments of society that are most vulnerable, like widows and orphans.[2] Yet the CC also wanted to protect the brother-in-law's right to property as defined by the title.

After mediating conversations with the widow and her brother-in-law, the woman decided to buy the roof from her brother-in-law so that strangers would not be living above her family. After all, she was a widow and should feel protected, and the brother-in-law's titling rights were ultimately respected because the widow paid for the property title. At the end of the dispute, both the brother-in-law and the widow were asked if they felt the decision-making process had been fair. They concluded that it felt fair (I-55L).

The interaction demonstrates two key points. First, as NIE predicted, the CC acted as a third-party enforcer with the authority and ability to use legal precedent to enforce adherence to the formal system of property rights in the camp. The handling of this case is illustrative of the way in which Fatah crafted the CC as a third-party enforcer of titles. An everyday woman from the camp felt that the place to go to resolve disputes was the local CC office, not a religious figure or camp elder. Moreover, the woman was not a member of a particularly powerful family or political group, yet the CC set about resolving the dispute. Again the system of enforcement was available to all, not just some members of society.

Second, even in a "Fatah-directed" enforcement system, Palestinians found a way to resist Fatah incorporation and protect their community norms of solving disputes through consensus. Hanafi and Knudsen (2010b) emphasize this point in their discussion of the provision of security in Nahr al-Bared. He argues that the Palestinian Armed Struggle Command, made up of members from a variety of factions inside the camps, "interacted and competed to negotiate the public good of the camp" (35). Clearly, the CC could have ruled in favor of the brother-in-law without "consulting" or "seeking compromise" with the widow. However, refugees from the community seated on the CC board felt that it was important to protect the value of the title as well as the broader community vision of a society that protects its most vulnerable members. They encouraged compromise between family members rather than simply enforcing the claim. As Scott (2009) predicted, the plasticity of the stateless group's experiences of doing business and managing claims afforded them an opportunity to adapt communal forms of enforcement within Fatah's formal enforcement system.

This system of formal property rights melded informal community practices of dispute resolution through consensus with Fatah's formal procedures for adjudication. The new system afforded Palestinian refugees a small measure of autonomy and protection from Fatah's complete co-optation of the community.

FATAH'S PREDATION OF SHARED RESOURCES

Though the new system of formal property rights safeguarded assets and offered Palestinian refugees protection from complete co-optation by Fatah, it also made the camps vulnerable to Fatah's political preferences and predation. Specifically, the tension between protection and predation was evident in the enforcement of property rights in shared resource sectors of electricity and water in the camps. Though most think of water and electricity as public utilities, in the case of refugee camps in Lebanon they function like a shared or common pool resource. Water and electricity are unique types of common pool resources called "mobile resource units" because they are not fixed (Ostrom 2000). Camps in Lebanon are given set quotas of electricity and water flows into the camps by the host country or private utility companies. Through the CC offices, camp residents must decide how to share the fixed amount of electricity and water. From this perspective, water and electricity inside refugee camps in Lebanon resemble traditional understandings of shared or common pool resources.

Palestinians negotiated the formalization of access and ownership to shared resources at the CC office in a similar manner to negotiations over private assets. Similar to private asset sectors, refugees had documents that were held in their names and were signed by the CC that entitled them to a certain number of amperes of electricity or liters of water (I-33L, I-34L, I-47L, I-53L). When homes and businesses were transferred between refugee residents, contracts explicitly stated that the new owner assumed access and responsibility for the electricity and water meters. In effect, refugees transferred electricity and water rights through the use of formal titles. The titles in appendix A are representative of titling systems in Beddawi and NBC.

Unlike private asset sectors, water and electricity access were not enforced despite the presence of enforcement tools like electricity and water meters to measure and monitor usage. Community norms acted as the only enforcement mechanism against potential abuse of water and electricity (I-47L, I-53L). In surveys, residents reported electricity and water theft by businesses as one of the top complaints of refugee camp life. According to surveys, the CC and Fatah did not stop businesses from tapping into pipes or circuits for extra use of water or electricity (I-5L, I-55L, I-6L, I-10L, I-16L).

An ice cream cone manufacturer that used large amounts of electricity brazenly noted that one of the benefits of working in NBC was "the low rent and the absence of electricity costs" (I-6L). He said, "I do not pay for my electricity at all even though my neighbors [families in homes] complain that my business uses too much" (I-6L). An aluminum manufacturer echoed the practices of the ice cream business: "I steal extra electricity all the time. I have an electrician that knows how to tap into the grid and rewire my access" (I-10L). A cement and tile manufacturer also stated that he used more than his contractually allotted title of water to mix cement for cinderblocks (I-1L). Interviews with the camp's electrician revealed that "it is quite easy to run extra wires and tap into the grid to steal electricity" (I-53L).

Fatah did not enforce preexisting limitations specified in titles on electricity usage with most businesses. Instead Fatah "encouraged" businesses to work during nonpeak usage hours between 12 A.M. and 6 A.M. to not overtax shared and scarce electricity and water supplies (I-6L, I-8L, I-9L, I-10L, I-16L). However, working at night introduced a host of new complaints that concentrated on the noise the machines produced and the disruption this caused for families at night. Most refugee families felt that businesses could afford private electricity generators and private wells instead of tapping into the community's limited shared resources (I-47L). Some businesses complained that the cost of the generators was prohibitively high and did not offer a practical solution to the problems they faced because complaints of noise would persist during the day too. In summary, Fatah did not enforce water and electricity titles (I-53L). Fatah knowingly permitted abuse in shared resources and allowed for predation.

ASSESSING EXPLANATIONS FOR THE LACK OF ENFORCEMENT IN SHARED RESOURCE SECTORS

Existing scholarship on common pool resource management points to several arguments for the difficulty in enforcing formal property rights in common pool resource sectors, especially in transitional settings. Briefly, many economists argue that a shift in the value of resources will cause a demand for property rights formalization, but enforcement is prohibitively costly in mobile resources like electricity and water. As such, conditions in transitional settings are not conducive to fomenting the economic demand necessary for formal property enforcement (Coase 1960). Second, sociohistorical scholars contend that even with sufficient economic demand, certain communities, especially refugees in a transitional setting, lack a shared community blueprint or model that could inform the formalization of property rights in shared resources (Acheson 1988; Yandle et al. 2011). Alternatively, New Institutional Economists contend that even with demand and a community-based model, the absence of a state with longtime horizons is unlikely in transitional settings and reduces prospects for institutional formalization (North 1995; North and Thomas 1973; North and Weingast 1989).

A longitudinal survey sample constructed between 2004 and 2012 tested existing arguments and found that they do not offer leverage in explaining the absence of formal titles in shared resource sectors in the Palestinian refugee case. In fact, Palestinian refugees had sufficient economic demand for formal property rights in shared resource sectors, had a historical blueprint for property rights pre-dating their 1948 refugee status, and had a political group with long-time horizons that ruled the camps.

THE INFRASTRUCTURE FOR ENFORCEMENT

Economists and environmentalists offered an explanation for local capture of formal property rights in shared sectors. It was argued that in the absence of critical market conditions like the presence of sufficient capital for investment, formalized property rights are unlikely to form or might be captured in the process of formation (Besley 1998; De Soto 1989 Demsetz 1967; Frye 1999; Markus 2012; Qian 2003; Sugden 1989). Formalization is a costly process, and in transitional settings the risk of investment often outweighs the benefits. Ostrom (2000) suggests that implementing individual rights to shared mobile resources is difficult because the cost of creating and maintaining an infrastructure for individual use of a common pool resource is considered prohibitively expensive for most communities. To effectively monitor and deliver such resources, communities need complex plumbing systems, electrical grids, and a special-ized labor force with the skills necessary to keep it all in working order. Coase succinctly noted that "the reason some activities are not the subject of contracts [property rights] is exactly the reason why some contracts are commonly unsatisfactory—it would cost too much to put the matter right" (1960, 39). Surveys addressed this argument by asking respondents and business entrepreneurs about the origin and timing sequence of their capital inflows.

First, increasing Gulf remittance flows into the camps meant that capital was present in the camps for investment (Smith 2012). Basic needs and services like shelter, health care, and education services were guaranteed by UNRWA for all registered refugees, so remit-tances gave families extra capital to invest in the camps (Schiff 1995; Smith 2012; UNRWA.org). Interview data suggest that remittances gave Palestinian refugees the capital necessary to invest in a variety of camp resources. In fact, refugee businessmen revealed that the number one source of capital for starting businesses and building homes came from remittances sent by family that worked abroad in Gulf countries and Libya that permitted Palestinians to work legally during the early 1970s. Most entrepreneurs used remittance sums ranging from $5,000 to $30,000 to start their businesses. During the oil boom in the early 1970s in the Middle East, Palestinian refugee camps also experienced a simultaneous boom in entrepreneurial spirit and business growth.

For example, a chocolate manufacturer in Beddawi noted that he and his partner worked together in Saudi Arabia for more than seventeen years to save money and start a business in the camps (I-12L). UNRWA small business loans, though less frequently used because of limited availability and budget constraints, provided another venue for capital. UNRWA's financial officer in Nahr al-Bared noted that seventy to eighty projects are funded annually throughout the entire camp (I-2L). Each project received roughly $3,000 (I-2L). Remittances were more important than UNRWA and Islamic bank loans in starting businesses (I-11L). Most of the money that caused market demand for property rights in the camps came from remittances sent by family members (I-2L).

The influx of capital from remittances caused a surge in the need for building supplies and shared resources like water and electricity because people could finally afford to improve their homes and invest in businesses. Many refugees opened businesses on the bottom floor of their camp plot and then built homes above the stores (I-3J, I-21L). These businesses were very successful. For example, the chocolate manufacturer in Beddawi had fifty-three full-time workers, most of them women, working two shifts a day.

In addition to the surge in remittances, entrepreneurs formed guilds and unions to express their collective business interests in the refugee camps. Most entrepreneurs wanted protection from Lebanese competition and low-cost access to valuable inputs like water and electricity (I-53L). Beginning in 1963, chapters of the General Union of Palestine Workers (GUPW) and other professional associations like the engineering and construction chapters organized around the interests of labor and business in Palestinian refugee communities throughout the Middle East (Brand 1988). Labor and business unions have a strong presence in camps across Lebanon even today (I-58L, I-80L). Contrary to the expectations of economists and environmentalists, camps in Lebanon had sufficient capital for investment and the infrastructure necessary to effectively monitor property rights in shared resource sectors.

THE PRE-*NAKBAH* BLUEPRINT FOR SHARED RESOURCE MANAGEMENT

Though some camps might have the economic conditions in place to formalize property rights, the sociohistorical literature argues that certain communities lack a shared history of formalizing property rights and that disparate notions of what ownership of shared resources entails prevent institutional formalization. In effect, some groups lack a historical blueprint or template to guide them in the process of establishing formal property rights in shared resource sectors (Yandle et al. 2011). Communal forms of ownership might preclude the community from establishing a private titling system to shared resources (Acheson 1988). Surveys assessed this causal argument by asking refugees about their pre-1948 relationship and understanding of property rights ownership in shared resource sectors. Did they own land, resource access, or private assets prior to their departure from Palestine? How did they establish ownership? Did they have titles? These questions gave insight about whether a preexisting blueprint for establishing a titling system existed among Palestinian refugees.

Prior to their arrival in refugee camps, the majority of refugees came from villages and towns in Palestine. Most Palestinian refugees in Lebanon had peasant backgrounds and worked in agricultural farming communities (Khalidi 1988). One hundred percent of the refugees interviewed identified informal individual titling procedures that governed rights to grazing pastures and water accessibility prior to the *Nakbah* of the 1948 war. Interestingly, they referenced different systems of law that governed resource management from their pre-*Nakbha* experiences. One business owner stated that his family adhered to Ottoman/Turkish rules of ownership with respect to shared resources. Some referenced British mandate law that allocated wells exclusively for Palestinian as opposed to Jewish settler use. Others identified local village customs with respect to water and grazing pastures. For example, many families had established grazing pastures that they passed down through families that were respected by other farmers in the community. In the event of overgrazing or disputes, local *mukhtars* or village leaders would use religious doctrine to settle disputes. Despite numerous accessible historical models for managing resources, formal property rights remained absent in the electricity and water sectors. I concluded that the sociohistorical perspective did not offer an adequate explanation for the absence of enforcement in shared resource sectors in the camps.

FATAH: A NONSTATE HEGEMON WITH LONGTIME HORIZONS

Finally, New Institutionalists contend that even with the right level of economic demand and a usable template for resource management, many communities lack the presence of a powerful group with longtime horizons that is requisite for institutional formalization in shared resource sectors. However, Fatah was clearly powerful and desired to stay in Palestinian refugee camps in Lebanon for the long term. From a practical standpoint, Fatah had few options to establish its authority elsewhere in the Middle East (Brand 1988). Following Black September in Jordan, increasing hostility in the Golan Heights between Syria and Israel, and Egypt's crisis of leadership following the 1967 war, Fatah had little choice but to situate its long-term goals in the context of camps in Lebanon.

The desire to remain in the camps was also reflected in the heavy infrastructural investments that Fatah along with the assistance of outside organizations constructed. Aside from CC offices, Fatah negotiated the introduction of sewage and plumbing systems and electrical access into the homes of every Palestinian refugee. Fatah convened formal meetings with a Lebanese electricity company in Tripoli, UNRWA officials, and international humanitarian donors during the early 1970s to develop the infrastructure for water and electricity flow into the camps (I-33L, I-53L, I-55L).[3] Through these partnerships and donor funds, Fatah was able to build a system of pipes and circuit boards that facilitated resource flow into the camps (I-33L, I-53L, I-55L).

Next, Fatah convened several meetings at CC offices with business owners, religious leaders, and other political parties to negotiate the formation of legal titles to electricity and water (I-34L). Fatah invited an array of local Palestinian political parties and refugee businessmen to a series of ongoing negotiations over property rights in an effort to consciously co-opt groups through participation in civil institutions. According to New Institutionalists, these conditions should have been sufficient for formal property rights enforcement even in shared resource sectors in a transitional setting. The unresolved tension between protection and predation evident in shared resource sectors indicates how transitional spaces, like refugee camps, are particularly vulnerable to powerful political groups that seek to control the political economic landscape.

THE TENSION BETWEEN PROTECTION AND PREDATION

Mair and Marti (2009) discuss the "dark side" of empowering local community stakeholders in Bangladesh's institutional void. In some cases, efforts to engage with elites "had unintended negative consequences such as strengthening patron-client relationships" and "perpetuating the exclusion of some of the ultra-poor" (Mair and Marti 2009, 433). Mansuri and Rao's (2012) World Bank report also warns against relying exclusively on the local level for institutional development because "entrenched elites, bribery, and fraud are as much of a problem in village life as they are in big emerging-market bureaucracies" (July 2012).

For example, Mansuri and Rao's study of a local licensing system in the forestry sector of Tanzania revealed that the local system of governance actually ended up raising barriers to entry for the poorest timber and charcoal producers while making them more dependent on town-based traders and powerful village elders (Mansuri and Rao 2012). It seems that marginalized minority groups are undermined by local elites at the substate level (Mansuri and Rao 2012). Though this evidence demonstrates the limits of local politics, it does not ascribe causality to *how* the local relationships and political motives capture conditions favorable to property rights formalization.

It was precisely Fatah's desire to consolidate political power that compelled members to permit and encourage predation in shared resource sectors. Though Fatah could have crafted formal property rights such that it could guarantee resources to all residents and monitor usage through the costly metering system (I-53L), political motives conflicted with the enforcement of titles in shared resource sectors. Fatah officials noted that their original intention was to allot every refugee resident and business with an equitable portion of the resource for an affordable price of roughly $7 to $15 per month (I-47L, I-55L). However, a retired Fatah official revealed that the party also wanted the political support of refugee businesses and unions (I-56L; Hanafi 2011, 35). "If Fatah denied the interests of local merchants on shared resource enforcement their political dominance in the community could have diminished" (I-56L). In effect, the property rights system in common pool resource sectors carried the interests of powerful local rent-seeking merchants as well (Thelen 2004).

Alliances between business elites and Fatah captured Fatah's enforcement mechanisms. Strategic negotiations between high-energy and water guzzling businesses that wanted unrestricted access to resources in order to compete with Lebanese businesses outside of the camp prevented the enforcement of property rights (I-21L). Powerful and prosperous merchants needed cheap or free access to large amounts of electricity and water to compete. An ice cream cone manufacturer said, "Listen, the only way I can compete with Lebanese businesses is because I have low rent, and low or no electricity costs" (I-6L). Low labor and input costs permitted camp businesses to undercut Lebanese prices (UNRWA 2009; I-21L). Whereas in private asset sectors businesses desired security with respect to their investments and willingly supported Fatah's formal titling system, in common pool resource sectors businessmen hoped to maximize profits by maintaining cheap or free unlimited access to water and electricity.

Businesses demanded free or low-cost water and electricity access in return for supporting private asset titles and providing political support to Fatah (I-56L). In exchange for the political support of powerful camp merchants, Fatah agreed to quietly and systematically ignore the exploitative practices of heavy energy and water guzzling businesses in industries like ice cream, chocolate, and cement manufacturing (I-55L). A camp electrician described the motives and political bargain inside the camps before 2007:

> Some businesses pay me lots of money to get them more electricity. I do not have a moral problem with it. I do not get in trouble with the Camp Committee. I receive payments from them [the CC] too. I need to make money for my family so I do the job. They [the businesses] need to make money for their families so they need the extra electricity for business. Fatah needs to give them [the businesses] electricity to keep in political power. Listen, if I see a family really struggling with not enough electricity. . . . Well, I will run a wire for them for free. This is what real life is like here. We trust in Allah to protect us. Otherwise, it is *fawdah* [anarchy]. (I-53L)

The strategic bargain between Fatah and powerful merchants mired efforts to enforce formal property rights in common pool resource sectors. Camp residents were aware of this political bargain. Though everyone resoundingly agreed that even the poorest refugees were guaranteed some water and electricity for a very modest price

(I-47L, I-55L), some businesses received more than their fair share. This resulted in constant electricity outages and extremely low water pressure for the average resident. One lawyer in the camp commented, "The Camp Committee has not been fair because they are politically corrupt. The Camp Committee represents the interests of a few powerful businesses in those [electricity and water] matters" (I-54L).

Fatah intentionally sacrificed common pool resource enforcement. The political agreement that prevented enforcement of resource usage was also reflected in discussions of corruption or *wasta*. For example, an iron manufacturer argued that the biggest problem for *certain* businesses in the camps was *wasta* (I-11L, I-12L). When pushed on what he meant by "certain businesses," he rephrased his response: "There is a game here in the camps. Either I get free electricity and maintain allegiance to Fatah or else I have to pay high bribe costs if I want get more than my fair share of electricity and water" (I-11L). A chocolate business owner noted that he had "unpopular political views" and his bribe costs were extremely high for electricity unlike those businesses that were strong Fatah supporters. To avoid paying bribes, he invested in several electricity generators to maintain his chocolate refrigeration system (I-11L). Lane notes that though political economic models might predict a powerful group to enforce property rights for their "economic well-being" and "maximization of profits," "the adequacy of such a model should for the particular case always be doubted" (Lane 1979, 84). In transitional settings, outsider political groups like Fatah have the power to engage in predation rather than protection in common pool resource sectors.

After the Cairo Accords in 1969, Palestinian refugees in Lebanon negotiated the formalization of property rights with Fatah. Fatah hoped to consolidate power in the camps and refugee residents hoped to protect their assets and community identity from outside predation. At meetings in CC offices, Palestinians converted their informal ways of enforcing property rights into a system that melded with Fatah's formal rules. The new system of formal property rights worked imperfectly. In particular, by entrusting Fatah with the authority to enforce titles in shared resource sectors, Palestinians opened themselves up to elite predation. For example, Fatah encouraged and permitted the abuse of shared resources like electricity and water among political allies like powerful merchants. Everyday camp residents were powerless to stop Fatah's predatory practices. In summary, the negotiated system of formal property rights in refugee camps across Lebanon reveals both the powers and limitations of locally contrived formal property rights in transitional settings.

5

RENEGOTIATING PROPERTY RIGHTS IN NAHR AL-BARED CAMP

The limits of locally contrived formal property rights in refugee camps across Lebanon were tested in 2007. Caught in the crosshairs of the 2007 violent conflict between Fatah al-Islam, a military and political group with murky origins, and the Lebanese military, Nahr al-Bared refugee camp was destroyed. Many Palestinians from Nahr al-Bared described the event as the "Second *Nakbah*" or "Second Catastrophe." For many it was the second most catastrophic event since the 1948 *Nakbah* when Palestinians first became refugees. For younger generations, it was their first time bearing witness to the devastation and chaos following dispossession from their "home" in the refugee camps. As a researcher, it was the first time I was able to track the evolution and renegotiation of property rights in real time.

While some might view the destruction of NBC's formal titling system in 2007 as evidence of the limitation of this study and of property rights in transitional settings more generally, it is clear from the interview data prior to 2007 that for many decades refugees in Lebanon buffered against instability, created a vibrant Palestinian political community, and engaged in institutional formalization that resulted in transformative growth for the camps. That was no small feat for Palestinian refugees given the terrible conditions in the camps in Lebanon. Certainly, there are limits to the powers of refugees in finding protection in transitional settings, but this does not preclude them from developing institutions for protection in all settings at all times.

Moreover, the destruction and reconstruction of Nahr al-Bared after the battle forced Palestinian refugees to renegotiate property rights inside the camp. The existing formal system of property rights negotiated with Fatah in the late 1960s crumbled under the military conflict. In its place, a new system of informal property rights developed that represents the latest iteration in the evolution of property rights in transitional conditions for Palestinian refugees. Palestinians used the general sense of confusion regarding the legality of owning property in the new NBC to their advantage. They embraced the ambiguity to protect the community and to avoid some measure of Lebanese domination. Palestinians strategically deployed pre-2007 titles and older informal Palestinian practices in enforcing property rights to meet the challenges of the Second *Nakbah* in NBC. This chapter unpacks the renegotiation of property rights between Palestinian refugees in NBC and the Lebanese military.

In the face of chaos after the Second *Nakbah*, Palestinians were once against thrust into political economic conditions not of their choosing. The international aid community agreed to rebuild Nahr al-Bared. The Lebanese agreed to the rebuild reluctantly, but hoped to block Palestinians from "owning" any land or assets inside the camp. Though the Lebanese asserted that Palestinians could not "own" their homes in the new NBC, Palestinians still hoped to protect assets through property rights and avoid Lebanese domination. They strategically pushed humanitarian organizations and engineering firms charged with the reconstruction of the camp to use pre-2007 Palestinian titles to map the structure of the new camp. In the new refugee camp, the Nahr al-Bared community sought protection through an ambiguously defined system of informal property rights. Though

Lebanon ruled with an iron fist and denied Palestinians formal property rights, refugees were able to keep their own understandings of property ownership alive and avoid complete Lebanese domination by using informal communal templates for enforcement. This new system of property rights was imperfect. In addition, it opened Palestinians up to a significant amount of Lebanese military predation. In the face of very difficult political economic conditions, Nahr al-Bared's refugees managed to protect their assets through an ambiguous system of informal property rights.

THE 2007 DESTRUCTION OF NAHR AL-BARED CAMP

I had the unfortunate privilege of witnessing the earliest bomb explosion in March 2007 in Nahr al-Bared when Fatah al-Islam rolled into the camp. Fatah al-Islam was a clandestine political group. It was clear that the group originated from outside the NBC camp community because they did not look, talk, dress, or behave like the rest of the community.[1] The Lebanese government hypothesized that Fatah al-Islam was the brainchild of Syria. They believe Syria masterminded the group's entrance into Nahr al-Bared and intended to use it as a proxy force to destabilize Lebanon and pull Palestinians into the political fray (Hanafi and Knudsen 2010b, 100). The pro-Syria Palestinian political group *Fatah Intifada* was the nucleus of Fatah al-Islam (Hanafi and Knudsen 2010b, 100). Though some Palestinians were part of Fatah al-Islam, they were not popularly supported. Moreover, Fatah vehemently opposed Fatah al-Islam and even offered to engage in battle against them with the Lebanese military (Hanafi and Knudsen 2010b, 107). It is generally believed that Fatah al-Islam originated from and was orchestrated from outside the camps. Using force, Fatah al-Islam took over a small building on the periphery of the refugee camp in early March 2007. Despite Nahr al-Bared's camp committee attempts to negotiate with this outside group, Fatah al-Islam refused to leave and threatened more violence if camp residents interfered with their actions. During the first week of their arrival, nighttime curfews were instituted and camp residents feared that the situation would worsen. I was forced to limit my research activities, remain inside my room in the camp when the sun set, and stay inside for fear of angering Fatah al-Islam. By mid-March, I made the prudent decision to temporarily stop my research project in Lebanon and pursue research in refugee camps in Jordan to bide my time. I planned to wait there until May to reassess the prospects for my return to NBC. However, no one expected that Fatah al-Islam would launch a surprise attack against the Lebanese military in Tripoli or that it would ultimately trigger a series of violent events that would destroy NBC. It would be another five years before I would set foot there again.

On May 15, 2007, Nahr al-Bared refugee camp was destroyed during a military conflict between Lebanese army officials and Fatah al-Islam (Butters 2008; UNRWA Report 2009). Ironically, May 15 also marks the exact day of Palestinian's first *Nakbah* in 1948. Neighboring Beddawi refugee camp remained structurally and politically unharmed. After a series of bombings and clashes on the ground, the conflict ended with the annihilation of Fatah al-Islam forces. On September 2, 2007, the Lebanese army declared an end to the hostilities, cordoned off the destroyed camp, and restricted access to military officials and approved Palestinian refugees (UNRWA Report 2009). Initially, it was unclear if the Lebanese government would permit the reconstruction of NBC because of the strategic location of the refugee camp close to the Syrian border and its proximity to the Mediterranean Sea for the Lebanese military. In addition, the reconstruction would be a costly project. In April 2008, Khatib al-Alami, an engineering firm, was contracted by the Lebanese government to conduct a preliminary assessment of damage and contamination (I-93L). Even during a visit to NBC in 2012, the catastrophic devastation of was evident as seen in figure 5.1.

After it was apparent that the camp was completely destroyed and required reconstruction, a large international donor conference convened in Vienna in June 2008 to decide the fate of NBC

FIGURE 5.1 Destruction in the Nahr al-Bared camp in 2012.

(I-57L, I-59L, I-90L, I-92L). In fact, Nahr al-Bared's Palestinian refugee noninvolvement in the conflict was a key argument supported at the Vienna Conference in 2008 that justified the reconstruction of the refugee camp (I-57L, I-59L, I-90L, I-92L). If Palestinians had not been true victims in the situation, the international community would not have been inclined to support the reconstruction of the camp. At the urging of the international community, the Lebanese government permitted the reconstruction of the camp (I-94L). In an interview, a Palestinian official commented, "Who knows if it [the reconstruction] is what the Lebanese really wanted? The international donor community demanded it as a matter of human rights and justice for Palestinian refugees. Lebanon was constrained to agree with the international recommendations at Vienna" (I-94L). On June 23, 2008, at the Vienna Conference, donors, Lebanese government officials, the Palestinian Authority, and United Nations Relief Works Agency (UNRWA) representatives voted unanimously to rebuild NBC and developed a "Master Plan" for reconstruction (I-92L). Reconstruction officially began on April 1, 2010 (I-92L).

Though the new NBC would be reconstructed to create an exact replica of the old camp (I-90L, I-92L), it would vary in one critical area compared to the old NBC. A Palestinian group, Fatah, had governed camps in Lebanon including NBC since 1969 through locally established camp committees (CC). However, after the destruction and reconstruction of NBC in 2007, the Lebanese military retained control of the new NBC camp and would administer rule at the local level. In fact, the Lebanese military asserted that it would administer the new NBC without the camp committees, abrogating terms of the 1969 Cairo Accords, thereby marginalizing the authority of Fatah and its governing structures (UNRWA Report 2009; I-80L, I-94L; Hanafi and Knudsen 2010a, 34–36). Hanafi and Knudsen (2010a) elaborate that Lebanon pushed for a military base to be built at the base of the new NBC and for a naval base positioned on the camp's beach. It was "a political statement to assert their absolute authority over the camp" (34–36). A member of the CC in the new NBC said, "Everything is now governed by the Lebanese military, not

the CC" (I-80L, I-92L, I-94L). A former Palestinian social affairs director in Nahr al-Bared said,

> In the old Camp Committee we helped to solve problems and serve
> the people. We listened to their voice and we helped to create hope
> with the protection of homes and businesses. But in the new Camp
> Committee, we have lost control. Fatah and the CCs are out. The
> Lebanese *mukhabarat* [secret police] are everywhere and they rule
> now. (I-56L)

In addition, the Lebanese would not permit Palestinian refugees to
"own" their homes or businesses in the new NBC. One refugee from
NBC poignantly described the shift in ownership rules after the Second *Nakbah* and Lebanese military rule:

> Of course, I want to return to NBC. But it will be very different there
> and most of all I will feel dispossessed for a second time. Do you know
> why? It is because I hear that I won't own my new place there, like I
> did before! I used to own a home in the camp that I was proud of—we
> worked for sixty years to scrape together a life. Now, we can't own,
> rent, or sell parts of our new home. (I-70L)

Unlike the new NBC, neighboring Beddawi remained politically
unchanged. Though Beddawi was strained with the influx of NBC residents after the conflict, Beddawi CC members expressed relief and
thankfulness that in the aftermath of the 2007 conflict, "the Lebanese army did not enter Beddawi affairs like they did in NBC" (I-58L).

FINANCIAL AND SOCIAL CHAOS FOR
NAHR AL-BARED REFUGEES

In the intervening years between NBC's destruction and the reconstruction of the new camp, NBC residents experienced complete
chaos. "There was a lot of anarchy following the conflict" (1-56L).

Refugees from Nahr al-Bared identified their financial and social conditions as two of the most challenging areas of life after the 2007 *Nakbah*.

In the immediate aftermath of the bombings, Palestinians ran from Nahr al-Bared to Beddawi. "I carried my niece, grabbed my jewelry, strapped on my purse, and ran to Beddawi for my life. It was frightening" (I-57L). For the first few nights, they were sheltered in UNRWA school buildings located in Beddawi (I-56L, I 58L, I-59L). They were welcomed in Beddawi camp "because Palestinians are hospitable to each other and wanted to support people from Bared camp. But [the residents] could do very little to help them financially because [they] had such scant resources to meet the demands of the influx of such a large population overnight" (I-58L).

After the initial devastation, UNRWA registered NBC families, gave them a rental allowance to find better shelter, and doled out new food ration cards (I-92L). An UNRWA official described the emergency response:

> The destruction was catastrophic and the demands on UNRWA were unprecedented. We had no established emergency plan to deal with such a situation. The first few nights, families slept in the schools, mosques, and even outside in the streets of Beddawi. On the ground, we developed a real-time plan to process the families and quickly get them set up in safe spaces. Aside from offering rental allowances, some families were relocated to the portable housing units. (I-92L)

Palestinians described the portable housing units as "barracks" or "cartons." In effect, they were trailers or shipping containers transformed into small apartment units. According to interviews, they were far from ideal spots because they were sweltering in the summer and frigid in the winter. "The walls were paper thin and people were stacked on top of each other" (I-79L).

Financially, most refugees from Nahr al-Bared lost everything when the camp was destroyed in 2007. Families lost everything they had worked to build since 1948. Families reported that in the old NBC,

Things cost less and we owned our homes and businesses. We could afford a pretty good life, all things considered. After the conflict, even with UNRWA allowance for rent . . . most were priced out of the market to rent even a filthy spot in Beddawi camp. In Tripoli the prices for renting were so high because the Lebanese were gouging us. There were so many of us that needed homes and there were not enough spaces. We lost everything in the camps and had no savings. Even though my husband has a good job with the UNRWA we can barely afford to make ends meet now. I suppose we are the lucky ones because we found a place to rent. Some families sat in the school shelters for months or they live in the *cartons* now. (I-74L)

Businesses also lost their shops and customer base following the conflict. For example, one former carpenter from Nahr al-Bared that relocated to Beddawi said, "In 2007 Nahr al-Bared's destruction ruined my carpentry business. For over one year I had no shop and no work. I used to have a big customer base that included Lebanese people from the villages. Everyone is scared to enter the camps now, even here in Beddawi" (I-65L). One refugee said,

Before 2007, there was a thriving economic market in Nahr al-Bared. I would say it was the most vibrant in the North [of Lebanon]. Things were better from all angles—low prices, high quality, good work, trustworthy people running businesses, and honest customers. After 2007 everything changed. The army is now controlling everything. Lebanese customers are afraid to enter into the camps so demand has gone really low for our products. The Lebanese moved their shopping elsewhere. Poverty levels seem much higher in the community than before. (I-79L)

Socially, the Palestinian community in Nahr al-Bared was fractured after 2007. Overnight the community scattered across Beddawi camp, Tripoli, and the adjacent Baqa'a valley to find shelter. The new living situation disrupted traditional family and community ties that bound the community together during previous conflicts (I-79L). For example, whereas one family once lived in the same building with the different floors and apartments representing different family generations, now the same family was strewn about different high-rise buildings in different camps and towns outside of Nahr al-Bared:

> I used to live with my Mom, my brothers, my brothers' families in one building. Everyone lived above our sundry shop where we sold candy and cigarettes to the camp. After 2007, my Mom found a tiny apartment for us to live in at Beddawi camp. One of my brothers and his family of six children lived with us. Ten of us were crowded in one bedroom and one bathroom. My other brothers found places to rent along the main road close to Nahr al-Bared. My Mom is too old to walk long distances so she can't visit her friends anymore. No one comes to visit us either. We feel alone here. (I-57L)

Another family that had lived in Nahr al-Bared since its inception described the social breakdown after the conflict:

> Everyone used to live close together. Our friends and family all had places next to us. We are now all spread out. We even used to have the cemetery with our loved ones close by to us where we could pray. Do you know we lost the cemetery and our loved ones graves were destroyed too? It is *haram* [a sin] what has happened to our community! (I-68L)

Though less talked about in public, one woman reported an increase in domestic violence after the conflict. She motioned to me to enter her home from her doorway. She invited me into her home to do an interview. After she removed her veil, I was shocked to see her horrific black eye. I suggested she visit the doctor and make use of UNRWA support groups that address domestic violence. In the meantime, she insisted that she wanted to tell her story:

After 2007, things got very bad between my husband and me. We don't live close to my friends and family. We used to be very well supported. Even though my husband didn't make much money, he made enough and we could live with his family. But since 2007, he hasn't found work for five years now and there was no space to live with his family when we relocated. He has started to drink and he comes home and hits me. Listen it is not like I am blaming everything on 2007, because we have had problems always. But after 2007, everything became bigger [magnified] between us. I felt we had both lost protection from our family and community. I am not so sure he would beat me like this or he could get away with it if we still lived in Nahr al-Bared. (I-77L)

A NBC sheik that was temporarily living in Beddawi camp summarized some of the social ills in the Nahr al-Bared community following the conflict:

We used to live next to one another. Our community was bonded and knitted to one another. We watched out for each other. Now we are geographically spread out, the community and the family cannot monitor, support, and enforce our values in the ways we used to. One thing I have noticed here is the high number of divorces among young women and men. We used to help new couples in the early years of marriage. You know we all lived with each other, we helped with their kids, helped them learn to solve marital problems before it got into a big fight. Now, these young couples live alone in UNRWA barracks and they have no support. Divorce numbers have skyrocketed. (I-72L)

In sum, Palestinians from Nahr al-Bared experienced financial and social chaos in the fractured years following the 2007 crisis. In addition to these challenges, Palestinians would face a new communal political threat in the form of Lebanese military domination.

LEBANESE MILITARY DOMINANCE OF NAHR AL-BARED AFTER 2007

The 2007 conflict drastically changed the local political landscape inside NBC. Strikingly, the Lebanese government asserted that it would administer the new NBC with top-down hierarchical military rule, abrogating terms of the 1969 Cairo Accords, thereby marginalizing the authority of Fatah and the consultative structures of the CC (UNRWA Report October 2010 and December 2010; I-80L, I-94L). The Palestinian Authority, UNRWA officials, Beddawi CC members, and NBC CC members lamented the changing political landscape in the new NBC (I-58-L, I-80L, I-89L, I-92L, I-94L). At the Palestinian Embassy in Lebanon, the representative in charge of the Palestinian-Lebanese Dialogue Committee noted that

> Lebanon considers the CCs illegal. Those committees have no power outside the camps and they owe their legality inside the camps to the Cairo Conference in 1969, which the Lebanese government has annulled unilaterally in NBC since 2007. Beddawi is ruling their own affairs still even though Lebanon does not recognize the local camp committee offices. Their annulment of the Cairo Accords in NBC is unprecedented. (I-94L)

A member of the CC in the new NBC said, "Everything is now governed by the Lebanese, not the CC" (I-80L, I-92L, I-94L). Camp residents in the new NBC viewed the Lebanese military as a foreign occupying force and feared the presence of Lebanese weaponry, checkpoints, and *mukhabarat* or secret police. One resident of the new NBC noted, "The new camp is frightening because the Lebanese army and the *mukhabarat* are everywhere. You are searched upon entry and exit. They control us completely through the use of force" (I-75L).

A woman from the new NBC said, "They clamped down on the camp border, it was once porous, but now you need special permission to get in and out. They [the military] rule us now" (I-78L). Another woman shared, "I have a joke now with my husband. When he fights and yells, I tell him, 'Be careful and watch way you say because the *mukhabarat* (secret police) is on the way!'" (I-57L).

Lebanese control even extended beneath, between, and above the homes and businesses inside the newly reconstructed camp. In an interesting interview with an engineer at Khatib al-Alami, I learned about Lebanese military restrictions on the size of sewer pipes beneath homes, the width of alleyways between structures, and the height of buildings. Prior to 2007, the camps were sprawling mazes with teetering buildings and open sewers flowing down paths. Navigating the camps, even in daylight, took an experienced resident. At night, even traveling to a home a block away required an expert navigator and a flashlight. Lebanese officials felt that the new camp should be better organized. Ostensibly, the new camp would be "better and improved" in its attention to health and sanitation conditions. Lebanese authorities justified the building restrictions as a natural outgrowth of attention to safety. However, the Khatib al-Alami engineer suggested that many of the construction changes were

> A reflection of Lebanese military security and an effort to control access and movement inside the camp. For example, sewer pipes have standard guidelines on size. They must be large enough so that an adult can fit inside for repairs and maintenance. A worker must be able to physically access and repair the interior of the pipes. Lebanese officials pushed for smaller sized pipes that men could not fit inside because they did not want Palestinians developing illegal tunnels for smuggling or military guerrilla efforts. (I-93L)

In addition, the engineer stated that most streets, lanes, and alleyways have standard widths to allow vehicles and pedestrians to safely traverse. However, the Lebanese wanted to create extra wide lanes and alleyways, "not for easier refugee access but for military vehicles like tanks to easily access the camps. Extremely narrow alleyways were not permitted because their absence would prevent Palestinians from easily attacking and evading Lebanese security officials" (I-93L).

Finally, homes and businesses were limited in their height to prevent aerial rooftop attacks from homes inside the camps (I-89L, I-93L). Additionally, a construction engineer in the new NBC stated, "The [Lebanese] government has strict rules about the new homes. There can be no more than four floors, there can be no balconies, you cannot dig too deep here, there can be no space for an underground structure to be built here" (I-89L). All of these examples paint a landscape of Lebanese domination inside Nahr al-Bared following the 2007 conflict.

FINDING PROTECTION IN AMBIGUOUS PROPERTY RIGHTS

Palestinian refugees in the new NBC faced a great challenge to protect community assets through property rights in the face of Lebanese military restrictions. There was a general sense of fear and oppression among Palestinians with respect to Lebanese rule. In a 2012 interview, a member of the CC in the new NBC asserted that "we do not control anything now. The Lebanese military controls enforcement in the camp. They [the Lebanese military] do not care about the voice of the Palestinians in the camps. They rule absolutely" (I-80L).

In these constrained conditions, Palestinians had different paths they could take in response to Lebanese domination. They could submit to Lebanese military domination and abide by strict rules that denied the community the right to own property. Alternatively, they could forge what Qian (2003) calls a "feasible path" to institutional protection that accepted the realities of the transitional setting but avoided total state incorporation and military domination.

Faced with two different responses to Lebanese domination, Palestinians opted for the latter option. They did not accept outside domination or remain "locked in" to the formal system of property rights that governed the camps prior to 2007. Property rights were dynamic. In response to the new ruling coalition of Lebanese military authority, Palestinians shifted their strategy of protection. They worked within the confines of Lebanese military rule and post-conflict confusion to craft a system of informal property rights that protected assets. They protected assets post-conflict by using informal claims and Fatah's titles predating 2007 in conversations with outside donors and engineers during the reconstruction process of the new NBC. This forced de facto international recognition of Palestinian "ownership" of homes and businesses in the camps. In addition, once residents moved to the new camp, they deployed informal communal enforcement practices to manage conflicts in the shadow of Lebanese domination.

Scott's (2009) study of the Zomias in Southeast Asia provides helpful insight into the Palestinian situation and how the refugees protected their assets and identity in the face of a more powerful group. "Zomia is and has been what might be called a 'fracture zone' of state making. . . . It has been peopled for two millennia, at least, by wave after wave of people in retreat and flight from state cores" (Scott 2009, 242). In the face of powerful states attempting to control their community, Zomias had a "choice between statelessness and incorporation. Within each of these choices there were, of course, several possible calibrated variations" (2009, 244). Zomias adopted an ambiguous and porous identity to adapt to the challenges of outside domination (2009, 256). As states tried to classify Zomias to create a population census or to formally register land claims, Zomias purposefully claimed a plastic and porous identity that evaded the state's system of control. Zomias pursued ambiguity as a political calculation to avoid incorporation and to preserve their community.

In a similar situation, Palestinians sought to preserve and protect their community assets by embracing and operating within the ambiguity that followed the conflict. Even if Lebanese authorities would not allow Palestinians to formally claim "ownership" of the new homes or permit them much of a role in the enforcement of the system, Palestinians could still play a significant part in devising the initial map of homes and businesses that outside aid and engineering groups would follow to construct the new camp. At the Vienna Conference, donors and international organizations agreed that reconstruction would only move forward in conversation with Palestinian refugees from Nahr al-Bared camp (UNRWA Report 2009). Though the Palestinian voice was destroyed in the CCs, the Lebanese military was obliged to allow community voice in the early stages of camp reconstruction. Under the guidance of international donors, the Lebanese military engaged in a structured community dialogue over the reconstruction, mapping, and division of resources in the new camp with the help of UNRWA and the Palestinian Embassy in Beirut. They created a working group called the "Nahr al-Bared Reconstruction Commission" or NBRC. "During the process of reconstruction, we had conversations about how the new camp would be set up. Residents were a part of the master plan. We wanted to preserve the village and kinship structure and the homes and businesses from before 2007" (I-89L).

In the aftermath of the catastrophic 2007 conflict, many Palestinians saved their paper titles that identified home, business, and resource ownership in NBC (I-80L). Those that did not still have their paper titles relied on neighbors to verify their claims. Once the international donor community and Lebanon agreed to rebuild NBC, the real task of reconstruction began. One aid worker noted, "It was unprecedented to rebuild a refugee camp. It was a chance to get things right. To create a better space that met the needs of the people but preserved the social fabric of Palestinians in NBC" (I-92L).

In the months and years following the conflict, each camp resident was invited to meet with the camp reconstruction committee, display their old titles (like the ones in appendix A), or to bring witnesses to verbally confirm ownership of a business or land, and sign off on a map that accurately depicted pre-2007 conditions. This was a long iterative conversation between refugees and officials that was called "the validation process" (I-92L). One member of the reconstruction team noted, "This was a messy iterative process. It took us two years to draft and finalize the maps from the homes and businesses. We used various stakeholders to draft the Master Plan" (I-90L).

A representative from the Palestinian Embassy shared a map of the validation process with me. The map shown in map 5.1 was the product of the sustained dialogue that took over two years to complete with residents. Careful examination of the map identifies the owner, location, and size of each camp residence or business prior to 2007. Neighbors on either side of the business or home represented on the map had to sign off on it. Engineers involved in the reconstruction created conversion charts that permitted residents a percentage of space in the new camp based on their old titles. This also extended to the amount of electricity and water that each resident and business would be permitted to consume (I-92L, I-94L). Businesses and homes were allotted specific access rights to water and electricity based on their needs like business type, key inputs, and size of family (I-92L).

Every single business that was interviewed prior to 2007 was destroyed during the Fatah al-Islam and Lebanese conflict. Despite their destruction, many businesses reopened in the new NBC with the assistance of UNRWA/Euro Commission small business grants and with the assistance of family remittances (I-81L, I-82L, I-83L, I-84L, I-85L, I-89L, I-92L). For example, former business owners from the old NBC were eligible for international grants valued up to $9,000 (I-81L, I-82L, I-83L, I-84L, I-85L, I-89L, I-92L). UNRWA used pre-2007 private asset titles to validate claims for business loans post-2007 (I-94L). Palestinian businesses in the new NBC were fighting to reestablish their businesses.

For example, an electrician in the new NBC chose to reopen his shop after 2007 because he received a $4,000 UNRWA grant (I-83L). He also felt that his business has been good for him because UNRWA's new NBC reconstruction teams are purchasing plastic electrical wire casings from him (I-83L). A bottled water producer also asserted that there was high demand inside the camps for his product (I-88L). In the new camp dynamics, these business owners

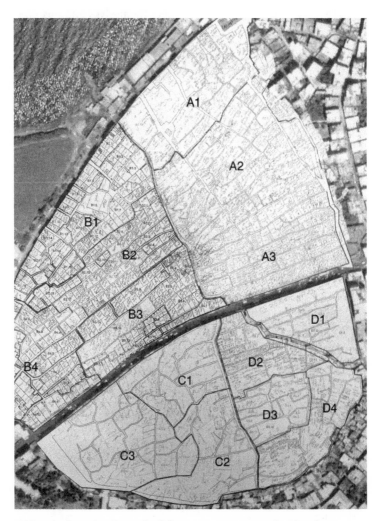

MAP 5.1 The Nahr al-Bared validation map was created with refugee input to reconstruct NBC after the 2007 conflict. During reconstruction, the social fabric of the camp was preserved because pre-1948 villages were grouped together. This map was provided to the author as a courtesy from the Palestinian Embassy in Beirut.

noted that they simply sought to protect themselves and push for recognition of their previous claims to businesses.

New businesses and residents were uncertain if they actually legally "owned" their new spaces. Importantly, they felt the newly reconstructed camp would preserve and knit together the community. Neighbors from before the conflict would remain neighbors in the new camp. Families and villages would stay close to each other. The prevailing sense of social order from before 2007 would be protected and enshrined in the new mapping of the camp. Palestinians were able to preserve the community's identity by using pre-2007 titles and informal property claims during the validation process. The new camp would "bring back to life and preserve our social kinship ties that were lost in the past few years after the conflict" (I-79L). Another family excitedly said, "We cannot wait to return and find the fabric of social and community life again" (I-68L).

In interviews, I pointed out that the international community was admitting de facto Palestinian "ownership" of assets in the camps by using Palestinian's informal claims and documents from Fatah's era of rule to map the new camp. When I asked if this meant that Palestinians owned property, most people evaded the question or said,

It is very confusing. (I-90L)

No one knows what this new system [of property rights] means. (I-91L)

Palestinians in the camps are in a very difficult confusing position. (I-92L)

Though the ambiguity was a logistical and bureaucratic nightmare for outsiders, officials, and researchers trying to make sense of property ownership in the camps, a closer look at the situation suggests that the ambiguity was a valuable tool for Palestinian protection. Like the Zomias, Palestinians used the general sense of confusion to their advantage to protect the community and avoid some measure of Lebanese domination and predation. One NBC resident and official described the confusion and Palestinian strategy at length:

> Listen to me, no one wants to talk about this because no one knows the answer. We *think* that the land in Nahr al-Bared was taken back by the government after 2007. Look, you can see they even built a military war hero statue for the bravery of Lebanese soldiers in the fight right in front of the camp. Clearly, they want to control this space. But then the international community puts pressure on Lebanon to rebuild the camp. I have no idea if they really wanted to rebuild or not. But when you asked me, "Does the refugee really own the home or not?" then my thought is that *I have no idea!* I do not think anybody really knows! The [Lebanese] government wants to own the homes and more importantly to own the people here. Of course, I am a Palestinian from here too and I know what will happen. You know too. We all know that Palestinians will make do in the confusion here and will do things under the table, informally. They will, and in fact have already started to, informally transfer apartments and businesses to each other without Lebanese or CC permission. (I-90L)

In the midst of the confusion, Palestinians crafted a system of informal property rights that protected assets. Aside from drawing the map of the new NBC, Palestinians deployed informal communal enforcement practices to resolve conflicts over property in the shadow of Lebanese domination. When there were disputes between Palestinians over property, they did not turn to Lebanese authorities or to the CC. Instead they used the network of pre-1948 kinship ties, village elders, and religious officials described in chapter 2 to resolve disputes. A steel construction worker that set up a new business in Lebanon after getting a loan from the UNRWA reported, "Since 2007, I no longer look to the Camp Committee for help. I certainly don't go to the Lebanese either. Our protection for the business and the home is with God and my neighbors. We do things within the [Palestinian] community" (I-62L).

A carpenter described post-2007 life:

> There is no security for us [Palestinian refugees] in the camps. The
> Lebanese military is everywhere. People say we should carry a
> weapon and not get involved in any politics or a religious party even.
> The absence of the Camp Committee is a problem. We have to just
> look to respected elders in our own community to solve any prob-
> lems with the business. (I-65L)

Another resident of the new NBC described the workings of the
informal system of property rights:

> I am one of the first shop owners to move back into Nahr al-Bared,
> everything is so new. I switched businesses to electricity and gas oven
> manufacturing and repairs. My place is located in the same place my
> shop used to be before 2007. The French government gave me a small
> grant around $1,000 U.S. dollars to buy machinery for my shop. I sup-
> pose things feel pretty safe here. Now, I don't look to the Lebanese for
> help or the Camp Committee. If I have problems now, I turn to older
> people. For example, I might go to the sheik. Otherwise, families sort
> out problems amongst themselves. (I-66L)

Within the confines of Lebanese domination, Palestinians found
protection through an informal system of property rights that
defined and enforced ownership claims.

PROTECTION IN THE FUTURE?

At the time I completed field research in May 2012, UNRWA officials
and engineering firms had partially completed the reconstruction
of the new Nahr al-Bared camp. In addition, the first wave of refugees from the old NBC had just moved into their new homes in the
new NBC. I took a tour of a gleaming new apartment that a family
seemed grateful to finally occupy after the years of stress and chaos

following the conflict. The arrival to the new NBC said, "I feel like I have my home again here" (I-86L).

Against all odds, Palestinians had recreated the structure of property ownership from the old NBC in the newly reconstructed Nahr al-Bared during the validation process of the reconstruction map. Moreover, they were using older established practices of resolving disputes using community enforcement mechanisms like village elders, family networks, and religious officials.

Still, the new system of informal property rights was imperfect because it existed in the shadow of Lebanese military domination. In the ambiguity of an informal property rights system, Palestinians coexisted with a much more powerful state neighbor. Informal property rights provided little formal protection from predation. The Lebanese military's primary resource, the use of force, was used to subdue Nahr al-Bared Palestinians if it was suspected that they were overstepping boundaries and undercutting Lebanese rules. On May 15, 2012, I visited Nahr al-Bared camp. It marked the fifth anniversary of the Second *Nakbah* of Nahr al-Bared and, interestingly, the sixty-fourth anniversary of the First *Nakbah* from Palestine. Palestinian refugees in NBC read aloud a proclamation that they would continue to persevere in the face of oppression inside and outside the camps. Then members of the community began to set fire to tires and chant in solidarity. The Lebanese military stood at the ready with tanks and guns as a reminder that their military power was a serious threat. In addition, it was suspected among camp residents that Lebanese military officials had an extensive network of local Palestinian refugees acting as informants.

> Some Palestinians will sell themselves for just about anything. It is pretty sad what someone will do for a smart phone. The Lebanese will give them phones and pre-paid phone minutes as payment for information about what the community in Nahr al-Bared is doing. We must always be careful. Ultimately, the Lebanese can clamp down on us at any time. (I-88L)

It was too early to assess the future of their informal system of ownership. Palestinian refugees in Nahr al-Bared are living in a precarious transitional setting. They have found some protection and autonomy from outsiders, but still occupy the penumbra of Lebanese military power. Nevertheless, the preliminary study of the validation process, reconstruction map, and desire to find protection through informal property rights suggested that Palestinians managed to navigate a precarious post-2007 political economic climate and claim some protection of their community's assets from Lebanese incorporation.

CONCLUSION

To know what it is like to live in Yarmouk, turn off your electricity, water, heating, eat once a day, live in the dark, live by burning wood.

—ANAS, YARMOUK REFUGEE CAMP (UNRWA, 2014)

Most houses have no doors or windows, and in the snow storm life became harder. We depend on radishes and lettuce and green things grown in the camp, but those food items had frozen. The water pipe exploded because of the snow.

—RAED'A, YARMOUK REFUGEE CAMP (UNRWA, 2014)

At 7 A.M. I walk one kilometer to get water for my home. I usually spend five hours a day collecting water, but I only collect water every five days because it is only available every five days.

—AZIZ, AGE TEN, YARMOUK REFUGEE CAMP (UNRWA, 2014)

The stories of Anas, Raed'a, and Aziz describe the Palestinian struggle to survive in Yarmouk refugee camp in Syria in 2014. In 2014, Yarmouk, a Palestinian refugee camp that was established shortly after the 1948 *Nakbah*, was under siege and UNRWA was able to bring food rations on only 113 days, averaging eighty-nine boxes per day over the year (http://www.unrwa.org/crisis-in-yarmouk). To meet the minimum needs of people, UNRWA should have delivered four hundred boxes of food each day (http://www.unrwa.org/crisis-in-yarmouk). As the protracted Syrian civil war pushes slowly toward a conclusion, Palestinians will have to renegotiate institutions in the refugee camps in conditions not of their choosing. What experiences will they strategically draw from to find protection amid chaos?

The Palestinian narrative and the theoretical findings from refugee camps in Lebanon and Jordan have direct links and clear implications for the Palestinian refugee community struggling to find protection in Syria today. Interestingly, Ali L.'s story that began this book closely parallels Palestinian refugee stories in Syria that describe the fear, terror, risk, and utter chaos of finding protection in the impossible conditions of violent conflict. Unlike the Palestinian voices from Yarmouk in 2014, Ali L.'s story traced the progression from chaos to order through the creation of informal and formal property rights. His story provides hope for protection in the midst of chaos. When the Syrian conflict one day reaches its end, Palestinian refugees will push for protection and will renegotiate the formation of property rights. It is my contention that Palestinians in Syria can learn from the most recent reconstruction efforts of refugees in Nahr al-Bared.

To make the connection to the current Palestinian refugee crisis in Syria, I begin with a brief review of results from Palestinian refugee camps in Lebanon and Jordan. After the review, findings are extended to Palestinian refugee camps in Syria before the 2011 civil war. In particular, a preliminary set of data I collected in Palestinian refugee camps in Syria in 2007 traces the formation and evolution of property rights in Homs refugee camp. Faced with another catastrophe when their camps were destroyed during the 2011 Syrian civil war, Palestinians are, once again, searching for order in chaos. To forge a pathway to protection and stability, Palestinian refugees in Syria can learn from the recent reconstruction efforts in Nahr al-Bared camp in Lebanon.

SUMMARY OF FINDINGS

First, Palestinians were not passive purveyors of their refugee camp conditions. Detailed interviews with refugees in seven camps across Jordan and Lebanon showed a vibrant community that actively sought to protect itself in the midst of chaos. Most Palestinians lost everything in 1948 and lived in abysmal conditions in the early years inside the camps. There were conflicts and intra-camp battles over resources, geographic positioning inside the camps, and political dominance. At the same time, entrepreneurial Palestinians created small businesses and slowly grew a customer base inside the camps and in neighboring villages. In the meantime, Palestinians felt they had to find a way to get along and looked to their pre-1948 village practices on property management and conflict resolution to anchor behavior in the refugee camps. The initial development of informal property rights was consistent with a "spontaneous order" explanation for institutional evolution. The community selected shared understandings of acceptable behavior and enforcement mechanisms like notions of family honor and shame to govern the camps in the absence of a state authority. In response to the 1948 *Nakbah* or Catastrophe, they developed informal institutions of property rights patterned on strategically selected pre-1948 norms of defining and enforcing property.

After a series of crises following the Arab defeat in the 1967 war, the 1969 Cairo Accords, and Black September in 1970, Palestinian refugees in camps across Jordan and Lebanon had to contend with new ruling coalitions. In Jordan, a huge influx of Gazans and Fatah's attacks against Israel prompted Jordanian authorities to clamp down on the refugee camps. Following the bloody Black September battles in 1970, Palestinians were forced to negotiate the formalization of property rights with the Hashemite monarchy. Jordan sought to dominate and control the camps. Palestinians hoped to protect their assets and avoid state incorporation. In response to the constraints of Jordanian authority, Palestinians converted pre-1948 methods of communal enforcement to gel with the Jordanian judicial system. The dual system gave refugees a voice and melded a Palestinian system of protection with a Jordanian model. Though it offered some protection of community assets, Jordanians often engaged in predatory behavior toward the most vulnerable subset of Gazan Palestinian refugees. Despite the shortcomings of the system, Palestinians strategically navigated the transitional landscape and managed to protect their community from outside domination with all odds against them.

In Lebanon after the 1969 Cairo Accords, Palestinian refugees negotiated the formalization of property rights with an outside Palestinian political group called Fatah. Fatah touted a revolutionary agenda that would activate and advocate for refugee interests domestically and internationally. Despite the positive aspects of their revolutionary slogans and local interest, they still sought to dominate and control the camps. In response to Fatah's new ruling coalition, Palestinian refugees negotiated the formalization of property rights at camp committee offices. Business owners hoped to create an efficient registration process. Palestinian refugees asserted their identity apart from Fatah using informal communal norms of compromise and family agreement to enforce titles. Though the negotiated system provided protection of assets and preserved camp communal behavior, Fatah still engaged in predatory practices with respect to shared resources like electricity and water in the camps. The limits of locally contrived property rights revealed the precarious balance refugees must strike between finding protection with new ruling coalitions and exposing themselves to predation by outsiders.

Finally, the 2007 destruction of Nahr al-Bared camp provides another example of how Palestinians negotiated for protection in the face of outside domination. They mapped pre-2007 practices of titling and enforcement during the "validation process" in which camp residents met with a reconstruction commission to establish property claims in the new camp. Despite their vulnerability to Lebanese *mukhabarat* or secret police, their ability to infuse Palestinian norms of protection in the confusing post-conflict space reveals the resiliency of communities in finding protection in transitional settings.

THEORETICAL FINDINGS

The results from findings in refugee camps in Jordan and Lebanon contribute to theoretical discussions of institutional formation and evolution. Contrary to strict path-dependent interpretations of institutional formation, my study shows that history might constrain but does not completely shackle the role of individual agency in building institutions. Palestinian refugees operated within strict parameters of outside control and rule. Their lives were often subject to broad geopolitical forces not of their choosing. Transitional settings, by their very nature, lack the stability associated with other political landscapes. Despite the limitations, communities can navigate the transitional terrain with a great deal of success and craft property rights that effectively define and enforce claims. Certainly, if conditions had been better, better forms of property rights might have developed. But as Qian (2003) notes, this is not a world in which communities should search for the "best" path, rather they should follow the "feasible" path to institutional formation.

Next, my findings in refugee camps suggest that the "feasible" path is not a linear one. As Thelen (2004) and Pierson (2004) hypothesized, institutional formation and evolution are iterative and dynamic processes. Institutions are not "locked in" but renegotiated in the face of shifting conditions on the ground. For Palestinians, critical junctures like the 1948 *Nakbah*, the late 1960s introduction of new ruling coalitions in camps across Lebanon and Jordan, and the 2007 reconstruction of NBC created moments in which the community was forced to devise new systems of property rights for protection. Rather than resign themselves to the domination and institutional system of the new and more powerful ruling coalition, refugees found protection when they devised strategies to meld their own Palestinian ways of managing property with outside groups.

Third, Palestinians treated past community experiences in managing and enforcing property rights as malleable identities that could meet the challenges of life in a transitional setting. A rigid understanding of communal identity would have had difficulty in adapting to shifting economic conditions and ruling coalitions in the conditions of refugee camp life. In transitional spaces where everything, including one's life, is under threat, then Palestinians strategically deployed parts of their pre-*Nakbah* ways of life, kinship ties, and enforcement practices to meet the challenges of life in the refugee camps. Like a lizard that changes colors to meet the challenges of its environment, a malleable communal identity permitted the community to camouflage itself in the face of dangerous and more powerful outsiders.

Existing approaches undertheorize the limitations of "feasible" property rights in transitional settings. When transitional communities, like Palestinian refugees, must negotiate institutions with more powerful groups, like states or military forces, they often risk endangering the very assets and identity they sought to protect from outsiders. In the Palestinian refugee case, outside groups wanted to control and consolidate power in the refugee camps. Though Palestinians negotiated compromises in enforcement mechanisms by infusing Palestinian methods of adjudication with state judicial systems, they were still vulnerable to predation. By institutionalizing the outside enforcers, they also formalized the dominance of an outside group that controlled more resources and power than the Palestinian community. Striking a balance between protection and predation is not easily achieved in transitional settings when one community is so much weaker from a political perspective than the outsider.

PALESTINIAN REFUGEE CAMPS IN SYRIA PRE-2011

These findings are extendable beyond Palestinian refugee camps in Lebanon and Jordan. In particular, there are a significant number of Palestinian refugees that have lived in refugee camps in Syria since 1948. Palestinian refugees in Syria are now doubly dispossessed because all twelve of UNRWA-operated camps have been severely damaged or rendered inoperable during the Syrian civil war. A scant few Palestinians have been able to flee to neighboring Arab countries due to entrance restrictions established in May 2014. Understanding conditions in Syria prior to 2011 sets the foundation for examining the community's prospects for protection in the face of this latest iteration of chaos.

The Palestinian story in Syria begins in much the same way that it began in Lebanon and Jordan. In the aftermath of the 1948 *Nakbah*, refugees from the northern part of Palestine, mainly from Safad, Haifa, and Jaffa, ended up in Syria. Following the 1967 war and the Israeli occupation of the Golan Heights, 100,000 more Palestinians fled to Syria (unrwa.org). Prior to the 2011 conflict, 526,744 Palestinian refugees were registered across twelve Palestinian refugee camps in Syria (unrwa.org). Of the twelve refugee camps, three are considered "unofficial." A number of so-called unofficial refugee camps were established over time by the host government to provide accommodation for Palestinian refugees. "In all respects, refugees in official and unofficial camps have equal access to UNRWA services, except that UNRWA is not responsible for solid waste collection in the unofficial camps" (unrwa.org).

To dig deeper into the transformation from chaos to protection through property rights in refugee camps across Syria prior to 2011, I visited Homs refugee camp. In 2007, I had the good fortune of collecting preliminary data there. Six surveys like the ones used in Jordan and Lebanon were dispatched in Homs. Admittedly, this is a tiny number of interviews. Originally, I planned follow-up trips to Homs, but political unrest, even in 2007, and the subsequent Syrian uprising and civil war that began in 2011 hindered such efforts. Nevertheless, the interviews suggest how property rights evolved in Palestinian refugee camps across Syria.

Prior to the outbreak of the civil war, 22,000 registered refugees lived in Homs camp (unrwa.org). The camp was established in 1949 on 0.15 square kilometers of land (unrwa.org). Most of the refugees that lived in Homs camp fled from Haifa, Tiberias, and Acre in northern Palestine in 1948 (unrwa.org). Homs refugee camp is located close to the Syrian-Lebanese border and is roughly 160 kilometers from Damascus. Like refugee camps in Lebanon and Jordan, the physical landscape of Homs camp was dotted with small businesses, construction industries, cramped homes, and tiny alleyways.

Results from my small number of interviews reaffirmed the pattern identified in other camps. In the main, the Palestinian community in Syria desired to protect itself through property rights. Notably, the pattern of formalizing property rights closely mimicked findings in Jordan. Like the Jordanians, formal property rights served as a critical linchpin in state-building and consolidation efforts for Syrian officials. Syria made a strategic decision to incorporate Palestinian refugee camps into surrounding areas (Hanafi and Knudsen 2010a, 30). On January 25, 1949, Law 450 was created to regulate Palestinian refugee behavior (Hanafi and Knudsen 2010a, 39). Law 450 provided for the administration of Palestinian refugee affairs and ensured their needs would be met through the establishment of Palestinian Arab Refugee Institute (PARI) under the auspices of Syrian Social Affairs and Labor Ministry (Hanafi and Knudsen 2010a, 39). PARI was later replaced with the General Administration for Palestine Arab Refugees (GAPAR) (Hanafi and Knudsen 2010a; unrwa.org). Syria further incorporated Palestinians into state structure through Law 260. On October 7, 1956, Law 260 granted Palestinian residents nearly the same status as Syrians in their ability to have equal rights in education, own property, have access to labor and employment, engage in trade, and commit to military service (Hanafi and Knudsen 2010a). Importantly, Palestinians were not granted national or political rights. In sum, Palestinians retained their Palestinian nationality while having many rights and privileges that everyday Syrians enjoyed.

Syrian officials established local camps offices under the control of the Syrian government through the branch of the Ministry of the Interior (I-1S). It was at these offices located on the outskirts of each camp that Palestinian refugees engaged in micro-level negotiations with Syrian authorities over the setup of a formal titling system (I-5S). In particular, refugees visited offices to record business transactions, register titles, report property disputes, and seek adjudication (I-3S).

The six interview respondents maintained that they developed formal property titles establishing ownership and protection of their investments inside the camp (I-1S through I-6S). An aluminum business owner explained property rights and practices in Homs refugee camp: "In Syria, the land is owned by the government. But we have the right to use the land and develop it as we see fit. I have a clear right to own businesses and homes in Homs camp. I have a title and if I want to sell my business I would change the name and transfer the business at the Palestinian Foundation Office" (I-1S). An iron business owner said,

> The Syrian government gave us land in Homs refugee camp to use for building on and developing for one hundred years. I have a title in my name that establishes my ownership of my business. I would go to the office of Palestinian Affairs with the Syrian Minister of Interior to change the name of the owner if I were to sell my place. It feels like we are treated, at least, equal to or better than Syrian citizens in terms of our rights to own here. The only thing I can't do is run for office! Hah. (I-2S)

Like the Jordanians, the Syrians played a central role behind the formalization of titles. For example, Syria's leadership sought control and co-optation of the Palestinian political identity and used the formalization process to shore up this endeavor (I-3S). Palestinian refugees, faced with the constraints of Syrian domination, crafted a system of property rights enforcement that melded their own forms of communal conflict resolution with Syrian rules to avoid total incorporation into the Syrian state apparatus (I-5S). A carpenter from Homs refugee camp explained the strategic use of practices from Palestine before 1948 in the new camp settings: "We lived in a farming village. I had papers that show my family owned the farm. If we had problems with defining or protecting access to the farm we figured them out within the family or with village elders. These are practices we knew how to use, even outside of Palestine" (I-5S).

Though the Syrians had police forces and courts that could enforce titles, Palestinians preferred to resolve intra-camp conflict concerning property rights using traditional community methods like village elders, religious sheiks, and family meetings to reach compromise, determine punishments, and seek restitution (Hanafi and Knudsen 2010a). "If it is a big case we would go to the Syrian courts because they do work, especially if we can't figure it out. But by keeping it [conflict resolution] within the Palestinian community we protect ourselves from too much Syrian involvement in camp affairs" (I-1S). From this evidence, we can see how Palestinians strategically melded their own past experiences of conflict resolution with Syrian rules to protect assets and avoid state incorporation. Prior to the Syrian civil war, there were similar patterns to the evolution of property rights across Palestinian refugee camps in Jordan, Lebanon, and Syria.

SYRIAN CIVIL WAR CHAOS

For Palestinian refugees in Syria, life was relatively stable and better when compared to Palestinians living in refugee camps across Jordan and Lebanon. The imperfect but feasible system of formal property rights inside the camps provided a good measure of protection until 2011. In 2011, during the early days of the Arab Spring Revolution blooming across the region, a small uprising spread like wildfire across Syria. Minor demonstrations began on January 26, 2011, in the city of Homs but were quickly dispersed by the secret police or *mukhabarat*. Many academics and policy experts thought President Bashar al-Assad of Syria would remain unscathed by protest because of his popular "nationalist" stands against the West, but by March 18, 2011, deadly clashes between protesters and the state flared again. What began initially as a small skirmish later ballooned into a violent and brutal civil conflict with a variety of local groups funded by international interests and the state regime vying for control and power. Caught in the crosshairs of the conflict, Palestinian refugees were thrust into a new chaos.

According to UNRWA, all twelve of the refugee camps have been either completely destroyed or rendered inoperable. In the early days of the conflict, a small number of Palestinians managed to flee to Jordan, Lebanon, or Turkey for safety and retained refugee services through UNRWA field offices in neighboring host countries. Astonishingly, a majority of the 526,744 registered Palestinian refugees remain trapped inside Syria today. By May 2014, Jordan and Lebanon closed their borders to Palestinian refugees from Syria. Syrian citizens could find refuge in many of those countries, but not Palestinian refugees. As of January 2015, there are 450,000 registered Palestinian refugees internally displaced in Syria (www.unrwa.org). Many Palestinian refugee communities like the one under siege in Yarmouk in 2014 are starved, frozen, subjected to regular bombings, and confronted with sniper attacks. For the time being, the international aid community and Palestinians are focused on the basic struggle to survive with adequate food, water, and shelter. Though the situation seems hopeless, an internationally brokered resolution to the civil war is inching forward. For Palestinian refugees in Syria, they will confront a new challenge to rebuild order and find protection amid post-war reconstruction. How will Palestinian refugees in Syria find protection in the confines of post-conflict Syria?

LESSONS FROM NAHR AL-BARED'S RECONSTRUCTION

In the midst of a civil war, Palestinian refugees in Syria can learn from the 2007 reconstruction of Nahr al-Bared refugee camp to guide their path to protection through property rights. Palestinians from Nahr al-Bared were a doubly dispossessed refugee community, just like the Palestinian refugee community from Homs and Yarmouk camps in Syria. After violent battles between Fatah al-Islam and Lebanese forces destroyed Nahr al-Bared in 2007, Palestinians struggled to survive in temporary living conditions in neighboring Beddawi refugee camp. Ultimately, the international aid community and the Lebanese government agreed to rebuild NBC. The reconstruction plan in NBC brought partnerships together between international donors, Lebanese officials, Palestinian officials, engineering firms, and UNRWA. Though this process was laborious and intensive, it worked in reconstructing a new NBC that preserved the social structure and informal property claims of camp residents. The success of the NBC reconstruction plan suggests an innovative pathway forward for the eventual rebuilding of Palestinian refugee camps in Syria. The NBC reconstruction process will be a useful template for Palestinians in Syria to follow because it remains a fresh collective memory in the international, regional, and humanitarian aid communities; it is an accessible blueprint because the Palestinian communities face similar constraints across host countries and most importantly it worked.

Though the reconstruction process resulted in the successful recreation of NBC, Palestinian refugees faced difficult parameters to finding protection of their assets and community identity. For example, during the reconstruction of NBC, Lebanon asserted that it would rule the new camp with military force and abolish pre-2007 Palestinian institutions. Moreover, Lebanon said Palestinians would not be allowed to formally "own" homes or businesses inside the newly rebuilt NBC. When pushed to ascertain who owned their homes and whether residents of NBC could pass their homes on to their children, there was no clear answer. The messiness and ambiguity was problematic for donors and officials, but Palestinians, like the Zomias of Scott's (2009) study, used the ambiguity to push their claims to assets forward and protect their communal identity from Lebanese predation.

Palestinian refugees from Syria can learn from the strategies of NBC residents during the reconstruction process. Within the strict parameters of Lebanese military rule, refugees capitalized on informal claims and remnants of titles from Fatah's era of rule to find voice during the process of camp reconstruction. Similarly, Palestinians in Syria will confront tight military restrictions during the reconstruction of their camps. The new ruling regime (or the new iteration of the old Syrian regime) will surely push to control and consolidate power in Palestinian camps. These confinements should not deter Palestinian refugees in Syria from seeking protection of their community assets and identity. Recall that during the reconstruction of Nahr al-Bared, residents converted earlier institutional practices into the mapping of the newly reconstructed Nahr al-Bared camp. During the "validation process" of reconstruction in particular, Palestinian refugees urged aid organizations and engineering firms to use informal refugee claims and pre-2007 titles to define the footprint and location of homes and businesses in the new camp. They brought in evidence of home or business ownership to substantiate their claims. For example, some brought in titles, photographs, receipts of inventory, and in cases where the family had no physical evidence of a claim, they used neighbors and community leaders to validate ownership. Based on their evidence during the validation process, a map was created to rebuild the new camp. In effect, outsiders admitted de facto Palestinian "ownership" in the new Nahr al-Bared camp by using pre-2007 claims and titles. Though the Lebanese military denied Palestinians formal ownership of assets, refugees strategically used traditional family and religious values to enforce protection of property in the camps.

Similarly, the validation process should serve as a critical point of leverage for the Palestinian refugee community in Syria. Using their own tattered pre-2011 titles, photographs, receipts of inventory, and informal witness statements, Palestinians in Syria can recreate physical maps of their camps. By preserving the physical and social structure of the old camp in the new landscape, Syrians should be able to protect their assets and community identity using traditional notions of honor and shame. Neighbors, family, and friends will remain closely tied to one another in the physical landscape of the new camp such that pre-2011 kinship bonds that fomented an atmosphere for trust and security in the camps can persist even in the uncertainty of post-conflict Syria. Though the new camp will be imperfect and the system of property rights will remain vulnerable to forces beyond their control, at the very least the Palestinian refugee experiences described in this book encourage us to reframe our understanding of transitional settings and realize a community's own potential for protection through property rights even in the most chaotic conditions.

APPENDIX A

TITLES FROM NBC AND BEDDAWI IN ARABIC WITH ENGLISH TRANSLATIONS

TITLE 1: NBC CAMP

IN THE NAME OF GOD THE MOST MERCIFUL

Palestinian Camp Committee; Phone #: 30/723095
Contract for Selling and Buying (One Seller and Two Buyers)

Seller 1	Buyer 1/2
Name	Name
Date of Birth	Date of Birth
Mother's Name	Mother's Name
File Number	File Number
Family Location	Family Location
Residency	Residency

The terms of the contract:

The seller: is selling an apartment in a building she owns, which has: four rooms, bathrooms, a kitchen, two balconies, all totaling 130 square meters. The apartment for sale is located: in NBC refugee camp on "New Street" and is located on the first floor of the building. The buyers have agreed with the seller to buy the apartment: for $8,000 American dollars and they have already paid for it in cash. The apartment will become the property of the buyer alone, they alone can benefit from it from trade or sale, and they can do so without the approval of anyone else. This contract was made with full knowledge and with sound body and mind. The sale cannot be reversed because payment has been received in full on: 8/8/2003.

Handwritten note: The two parties have agreed that the electricity and water meters and pumps are jointly owned.

Seller 1:   Buyer 1:   Buyer 2:

Stamp: There is a stamp in the bottom left-hand corner that contains a symbol of the Palestinian CC and states that the "Agreement is authentic" by the Palestinian CC in NBC.

CONTRACT OF SALE

House-Warehouse
First Party: _____ Second Party: _____

I. Item One:

The First Party gives up the house/warehouse in sector to the Second Party

The House/Warehouse's location is determined by the following boundaries from:

The North: _____

The South: _____

The East: _____

The West: _____

It is licensed in UNRWA records as number: _____

In exchange for a monetary sum of: _____

The House/Warehouse is composed of: _____

اللجنة الشعبيّة الفلسطينيّة

عقـــد بيـــع

ــمخيّم البّداويـ ــ

منـزل – مخـزنٌ

الفَريق الأوّلَ : .... الفريق الثاني : ....

• المادة الأولى :

يتنازل الفريق الأول للفريق الثاني عن المنزل – المخزن في مخيم البداوي في قطاع ....
الذي يحده من الجهة :
الشمالية : ....
الجنوبية : ....
الشرقية : ....
الغربية : ....

والمجاز في سجلات الأنروا رقم .... وذلك لقاء مبلغ وقدره.............
والمنزل مكوّن من : ....

• المادة الثانية :

يستلم الفريق الثاني المنزل المذكور من الفريق الأول بعد أن يدفع له المبلغ المتفق عليه عدًّا ونقدًا

• المادة الثالثة :

يلتزم الفريق الثاني بتسديد كافة الرسوم المتوجبة على المنزل المذكور من مياه وكهرباء وغيرها .

• المادة الرابعة :

حرّر هذا العقد بتاريخ .... على أربع نسخ :
١ـ نسخة للفريق الأول
٢ـ نسخة للفريق الثاني
٣ـ نسخة تحفظ في سجلات القطاع " مخيم البداوي " .
٤ـ نسخة تحفظ في ملفات اللجنة الشعبية الفلسطينية " مخيم البداوي " .
٥ـ

الفريق الأوّل :........................ الفريق الثاني : ....
الشاهد-الأول : .... الشاهد الثاني : ....
شوهد وصدّق شوهد وصدّق

الكفاح المسلح الفلسطيني مخيم البداوي اللجنة الشعبية الفلسطينية مخيم البداوي
مسؤول القطاع : أمين السر : أبو خالد

TITLE 2: PALESTINIAN PEOPLE'S COMMITTEE; BEDDAWI CAMP

II. Item Two:

The Second Party will receive the aforementioned House/Warehouse from the First Party after the First Party receives the monetary sum previously agreed upon.

III. Item Three:

The Second Party is committed to paying all the necessary fees for the house, including water, electricity, and similar matters.

IV. Item Four:

This contract has been released on _____ with four copies:

    A copy for the First Party
    A copy for the Second Party
    A copy to be saved in the files of the "Beddawi Camp" Sector
    A copy to be saved in the files of the Palestinian People's Committee under "Beddawi Camp"

The First Party: _____
The Second Party: _____
The First Witness: _____
The Second Witness: _____

Witnessed and Notarized:
The Palestinian Armed Resistance of Beddawi Camp
The Sector Official: _____
Witnessed and Notarized: _____
The Palestinian People's Committee Beddawi Camp
The Secretary: Abu Khaled

APPENDIX B

RESEARCH METHODS

A complete list of interviews that identify occupation, affiliation, and the location and date of the interview is provided below. In accordance with IRB regulations, personal names are omitted to protect the identities of the informants.

INTERVIEWS IN JORDAN

2004

I-1J: Director, Department of Refugee Affairs, PLO, Amman, June 27, 2004.

I-2J: Chief Field Officer, UNRWA, Relief and Social Services, Amman, June 30, 2004.

I-3J: Chief Information Officer, UNRWA, Amman, June 30, 2004.

2005

I-4J: Business owner, Iron production, Baqa'a camp, May 17, 2005.

I-5J: Business owner, Iron production, Baqa'a camp, May 17, 2005.

I-6J: Business owner, Iron and aluminum production, Baqa'a camp, May 17, 2005.

I-7J: Business owner, Carpentry and furniture retail, Baqa'a camp, May 18, 2005.

I-8J: Business owner, Carpentry, Baqa'a camp, May 18, 2005.

I-9J: Business owner, Carpentry, Baqa'a camp, May 18, 2005.

I-10J: Business owner, Cinderblocks, Baqa'a camp, May 18, 2005.

I-11J: Business owner, Cinderblocks, Baqa'a camp, May 18, 2005.

I-12J: Business owner, Glass, Baqa'a camp, May 19, 2005.

I-13J: Business owner, Glass, Baqa'a camp, May 19, 2005.

I-14J: Business owner, Glass, Baqa'a camp, May 19, 2005.

I-15J: Business owner, Carpentry, Zarqa camp, May 20, 2005.

I-16J: Business owner, Iron, Zarqa camp, May 20, 2005.

I-17J: Business owner, Iron, Zarqa camp, May 20, 2005.

I-18J: Business owner, Carpentry, Zarqa camp, May 20, 2005.

I-19J: Business owner, Iron, Zarqa camp, May 20, 2005.

I-20J: Business owner, Carpentry, Zarqa camp, May 21, 2005.

I-21J: Business owner, Iron, Zarqa camp, May 25, 2005.

I-22J: Business owner, Iron, Zarqa camp, May 25, 2005.

I-23J: Business owner, Glass, Zarqa camp, May 25, 2005.

I-24J: Business owner, Glass, Zarqa camp, May 26, 2005.

I-25J: Business owner, Cinderblocks, Zarqa camp, May 26, 2005.

I-26J: Business owner, Glass, Zarqa camp, May 26, 2005.

I-27J: Business owner, Cinderblocks, Zarqa camp, May 26, 2005.

I-30J: Business owner, Cinderblocks, Zarqa camp, May 27, 2005.

I-31J: Business owner, Carpentry, Wihdat camp, June 1, 2005.

I-32J: Business owner, Aluminum and glass, Wihdat camp, June 1, 2005.

I-33J: Business owner, Iron, Wihdat camp, June 1, 2005.

I-34J: Business owner, Glass and carpentry, Wihdat camp, June 1, 2005.

I-35J: Business owner, Iron, Wihdat camp, June 2, 2005.

I-36J: Business owner, Carpentry, Wihdat camp, June 2, 2005.

I-37J: Business owner, Carpentry, Wihdat camp, June 2, 2005.

I-38J: Business owner, Iron, Wihdat camp, June 2, 2005.

I-39J: Business owner, Glass, Wihdat camp, June 2, 2005.

I-40J: Business owner, Iron, Wihdat camp, June 3, 2005.

I-41J: Business owner, Iron, Wihdat camp, June 3, 2005.

I-42J: Business owner, Glass, Wihdat camp, June 3, 2005.

I-43J: Business owner, Cinderblock and tile, Wihdat camp, June 3, 2005.

I-44J: Business owner, Cinderblock and tile, Wihdat camp, June 3, 2005.

I-45J: Business owner, Carpentry, Irbid camp, June 7, 2005.

I-46J: Business owner, Carpentry, Irbid camp, June 7, 2005.

I-47J: Business owner, Carpentry, Irbid camp, June 7, 2005.

I-48J: Business owner, Carpentry, Irbid camp, June 7, 2005.

I-49J: Business owner, Iron, Irbid camp, June 7, 2005.

I-50J: Business owner, Iron, Irbid camp, June 8, 2005.

I-51J: Business owner, Iron, Irbid camp, June 8, 2005.

I-52J: Business owner, Cinderblock, Irbid camp, June 8, 2005.

I-53J: Business owner, Tile and cinderblock, Irbid camp, June 8, 2005.

I-54J: Business owner, Tile, Irbid camp, June 8, 2005.

I-55J: Business owner, Glass, Irbid camp, June 9, 2005.

I-56J: Business owner, Tile and cinderblock, Irbid camp, June 9, 2005.

I-57J: Business owner, Glass and aluminum framing, Irbid camp, June 9, 2005.

I-58J: Business owner, Iron, Marka camp, June 15, 2005.

I-59J: Business owner, Carpentry, Marka camp, June 15, 2005.

I-60J: Business owner, Iron, Marka camp, June 15, 2005.

I-61J: Business owner, Iron, Marka camp, June 15, 2005.

I-62J: Business owner, Glass, Marka camp, June 15, 2005.

I-63J: Business owner, Carpentry, Marka camp, June 16, 2005.

I-64J: Business owner, Glass, Marka camp, June 16, 2005.

I-65J: Business owner, Tile and cinderblock, Marka camp, June 16, 2005.

I-66J: Business owner, Tile and cinderblock, Marka camp, June 16, 2005.

I-67J: Business owner, Carpentry and wood distribution, Marka camp, June 16, 2005.

2007

I-68J: Business owner, Iron, Baqa'a camp, March 29, 2007.

I-69J: Business owner, Iron, Baqa'a camp, March 29, 2007.

I-70J: Business owner, Carpentry and iron, Baqa'a camp, March 29, 2007.

I-71J: Business owner, Iron, Baqa'a camp, March 29, 2007.

I-72J: Sheikh, Baqa'a camp, March 29, 2007.

I-73J: Business owner, Tile and iron, Baqa'a camp, March 30, 2007.

I-74J: Business owner, Aluminum, Baqa'a camp, March 30, 2007.

I-75J: Business owner, Carpentry, Baqa'a camp, March 30, 2007.

I-76J: Business owner, Tile and cinderblock, Baqa'a camp, March 30, 2007.

I-77J: Business owner, Carpentry, Baqa'a camp, March 31, 2007.

I-78J: Business owner, Carpentry, Baqa'a camp, March 31, 2007.

I-79J: Former Minister of Electricity, Phone interview in Amman, April 4, 2007.

I-80J: Business owner, Iron and steel production, Wihdat camp, April 5, 2007.

I-81J: Business owner, Carpentry, Wihdat camp, April 5, 2007.

I-82J: Business owner, Iron and steel works, Wihdat camp, April 5, 2007.

I-83J: Business owner, Aluminum, Wihdat camp, April 5, 2007.

I-84J: Business owner, Construction material trader, Wihdat camp, April 6, 2007.

I-85J: Business owner, Glass manufacturing and design, Wihdat camp, April 6, 2007.

I-86J: Business owner, Carpentry, Wihdat camp, April 6, 2007.

I-87J: Business owner, Iron, Wihdat camp, April 7, 2007.

I-88J: Business owner, Building supplies, Wihdat camp, April 7, 2007.

I-89J: Business owner, Iron, Jerash camp, April 11, 2007.

I-90J: Business owner, Iron, Jerash camp, April 11, 2007.

I-91J: Business owner, Carpentry, Jerash camp, April 11, 2007.

I-92J: Business owner, Cinderblock and tile, Jerash camp, April 12, 2007.

I-93J: Business owner, Iron and steel, Jerash camp, April 12, 2007.

I-94J: Business owner, Metal works, Jerash camp, April 12, 2007.

I-95J: Business owner, Aluminum, Jerash camp, April 12, 2007.

I-96J: Business owner, Carpentry with specialization in framing structures, Jerash camp, April 13, 2007.

I-97J: Business owner, Iron and steel, Jerash camp, April 13, 2007.

INTERVIEWS IN LEBANON

2004

I-1L: Business owner, Tile and concrete block factory, Nahr al-Bared camp, July 4, 2004.

I-2L: Head Officer, Financial Assistance to Businesses, UNRWA, Nahr al-Bared camp, July 5, 2004.

I-3L: Camp Leader, UNRWA, Nahr al-Bared camp, July 5, 2004.

I-4L: Lawyer, Nahr al-Bared camp, July 8, 2004.

I-5L: Area Officer, Baqa'a Northern Lebanon region, UNRWA, Tripoli, July 8, 2004.

I-6L: Business owner, Ice cream cones, Nahr al-Bared camp, July 10, 2004.

I-7L: Business owner, Chocolate factory, Nahr al-Bared camp, July 10, 2004.

I-8L: Business owner, Ice cream production and retail, Nahr al-Bared camp, July 10, 2004.

I-9L: Business owner, Ice cream production and retail, Nahr al-Bared camp, July 11, 2004.

I-10L: Business owner, Aluminum, Nahr al-Bared camp, July 11, 2004.

I-11L: Business owner, Iron, Bedawi camp, July 12, 2004.

I-12L: Business owner, Chocolate factory, Bedawi camp, July 12, 2004.

I-13L: Business owner, Tile factory, Bedawi camp, July 12, 2004.

I-14L: Business owner, Tile and cinderblock production, Bedawi camp, July 12, 2004.

I-15L: Business owner, Carpentry and furniture retail, Bedawi camp, July 12, 2004.

I-16L: Business owner, Ice cream production, Bedawi camp, July 12, 2004.

I-17L: Business owner, Chocolate factory, Bedawi camp, July 12, 2004.

I-18L: Business owner, Carpentry and furniture retail, Nahr al-Bared camp, July 13, 2004.

I-19L: Business owner, Steel production, Nahr al-Bared camp, July 13, 2004.

I-20L: Field Leader, National Association for Vocation training school, Beirut, July 15, 2004.

I-21L: Chief Public Information Officer, UNRWA, Beirut, July 15, 2004.

I-22L: Business owner, Carpentry, al-Buss camp, July 17, 2004.

I-23L: Leader/Head, Popular Camp Committee, al-Buss camp, July 17, 2004.

I-24L: Head, Najda Vocational Center, al-Buss camp, July 17, 2004.

I-25L: Camp Leader, UNRWA, al-Buss camp, July 17, 2004.

I-26L: Popular Camp Committee Leader, Rashidieh camp, July 18, 2004.

I-27L: Business owner, Iron, al-Buss camp, July 19, 2004.

I-28L: Business owner, Iron, Rashidieh camp, July 19, 2004.

I-29L: Area Officer, Tyre region, UNRWA, Tyre, July 19, 2004.

I-30L: Leader, Najda Micro-Credit office, Rashidieh camp, July 19, 2004.

I-31L: Business owner, Ice cream production, Rashidieh camp, July 19, 2004.

I-32L: Business owner, Ice cream production, al-Buss camp, July 20, 2004.

2007

I-33L: Popular Camp Committee, meeting with entire committee, Nahr al-Bared camp, February 26, 2007.

I-34L: Committee Member, Water and electricity expert, Nahr al-Bared camp, February 26, 2007.

I-35L: Business owner, Carpentry, Nahr al-Bared camp, February 26, 2007.

I-36L: Business owner, Steel, Nahr al-Bared camp, February 26, 2007.

I-37L: Business owner, Aluminum, Nahr al-Bared camp, February 26, 2007.

I-38L: Business owner, Cinderblock and tile, Bedawi camp, February 27, 2007.

I-39L: Business owner, Cement and cinderblock, Bedawi camp, February 27, 2007.

I-40L: Business owner, Carpentry, Bedawi camp, February 27, 2007.

I-41L: Business owner, Carpentry, Bedawi camp, February 27, 2007.

I-42L: Business owner, Aluminum, Bedawi camp, February 28, 2007.

I-43L: Business owner, Aluminum, Bedawi camp, February 28, 2007.

I-44L: Business owner, Glass, Bedawi camp, February 28, 2007.

I-45L: Business owner, Tile, Nahr al-Bared camp, March 2, 2007.

I-46L: Business owner, Iron, Nahr al-Bared camp, March 2, 2007.

I-47L: Meeting with a family, Nahr al-Bared camp, March 3, 2007.

I-48L: Fatah party member and party accountant, Nahr al-Bared camp, March 4, 2007.

I-49L: Business owner, Aluminum, Nahr al-Bared camp, March 7, 2007.

I-50L: Business owner, Plaster and wall décor, Nahr al-Bared camp, March 7, 2007.

I-51L: Business owner, Tile and cinderblock, Nahr al-Bared camp, March 7, 2007.

I-52L: Business owner, Tile, Nahr al-Bared camp, March 7, 2007.

I-53L: Camp Electrician, Nahr al-Bared camp, March 12, 2007.

I-54L: Lawyer, Nahr al-Bared camp, March 12, 2007.

I-55L: Popular Camp Committee, meeting with entire committee, Bedawi camp, March 17, 2007.

2012

I-56L: Retired Fatah official, Nahr al-Bared camp, May 16, 2012.

I-57L: Female Nahr al-Bared resident and UNRWA data collector, May 16, 2012.

I-58L: Camp Committee collective interview, five members present out of twenty-three, Beddawi camp, May 16, 2012.

I-59L: UNRWA Information Officer, Beddawi camp, May 16, 2012.

I-60L: Business owner, Iron and steel, Beddawi camp, May 17, 2012.

I-61L: Business owner, Carpentry, Beddawi camp, May 17, 2012.

I-62L: Business owner, Steel, Beddawi camp, May 17, 2012.

I-63L: Construction worker in Nahr al-Bared rebuild, Beddawi camp, May 17, 2012.

I-64L: Business owner, Carpentry and painting, Beddawi camp, May 17, 2012.

I-65L: Business owner, Carpentry, Beddawi camp, May 17, 2012.

I-66L: Business owner, Gas installation and electrician, Beddawi camp, May 17, 2012.

I-67L: Business owner, Tile and marble, Beddawi camp, May 18, 2012.

I-68L: Nahr al-Bared relocated family, Beddawi camp, May 18, 2012.

I-69L: Nahr al-Bared former business owner, Beddawi camp, May 18, 2012.

I-70L: Nahr al-Bared relocated family, Beddawi camp, May 18, 2012.

I-71L: Medical doctor that worked in Nahr al-Bared, Beddawi camp, May 18, 2012.

I-72L: Sheikh, Beddawi camp, May 18, 2012.

I-73L: Nahr al-Bared family, Beddawi camp, May, 18, 2012.

I-74L: Nahr al-Bared family, Beddawi camp, May 18, 2012.

I-75L: Nahr al-Bared woman, Beddawi camp, May 18, 2012.

I-76L: Nahr al-Bared woman, Beddawi camp, May 18, 2012.

I-77L: Nahr al-Bared woman, Beddawi camp, May, 18, 2012.

I-78L: Nahr al-Bared family, new Nahr al-Bared camp, May 19, 2012.

I-79L: Nahr al-Bared sheikh, new Nahr al-Bared camp, May 19, 2012.

I-80L: Nahr al-Bared Camp Committee, sixteen out of thirty-four members present, new Nahr al-Bared camp, May 19, 2012.

I-81L: Business owner, Carpentry, new Nahr al-Bared camp, May 19, 2012.

I-82L: Business owner, Electricity, new Nahr al-Bared camp, May 19, 2012.

I-83L: Business owner, Bathroom construction and tile, new Nahr al-Bared camp, May 19, 2012.

I-84L: Business owner, Iron and steel, new Nahr al-Bared camp, May 20, 2012.

I-85L: Business owner, Iron, new Nahr al-Bared camp, May 20, 2012.

I-86L: Business owner, Recycling construction materials, new Nahr al-Bared camp, May 20, 2012.

I-87L: Business owner, Construction material—sand, tile, cement, steel, new Nahr al-Bared camp, May 20, 2012.

I-88L: Business owner, Bottled water production, new Nahr al-Bared camp, May 20, 2012.

I-89L: UNRWA Reconstruction Engineer, new Nahr al-Bared camp, May 21, 2012.

I-90L: UNRWA Northern Lebanon field office, new Nahr al-Bared reconstruction officer, May 23, 2012.

I-91L: Nahr al-Bared historian, Tripoli, May 24, 2012.

I-92L: UNRWA Lebanon field office, Chief Information Officer, Beirut, May 29, 2012.

I-93L: Engineering firm, Nahr al-Bared reconstruction liaison to Lebanon government, Beirut, May 29, 2012.

I-94L: Palestinian Embassy representative, Chief Diplomat to the Nahr al-Bared reconstruction project in the Palestinian-Lebanese Dialogue Committee, May 31, 2012.

I-95L: Head of Beddawi camp, July 6, 2004.

I-96L: Former Nahr al-Bared resident, May 31, 2012.

INTERVIEWS IN SYRIA

2007

I-1S: Business owner, Aluminum, Homs camp, March 8, 2007.

I-2S: Business owner, Iron, Homs camp, March 8, 2007.

I-3S: Business owner, Carpentry, Homs camp, March 9, 2007.

I-4S: Business owner, Glass production and design, Homs camp, March 9, 2007.

I-5S: Business owner, Tile and cement production, Homs camp, March 9, 2007.

I-6S: Business owner, Carpentry, Homs camp, March 9, 2007.

VERBAL SCRIPT FOR OBTAINING INFORMED ORAL CONSENT

(Consent Documentation Waived)

"Hello, my name is Professor (Dr.) *Nadya Hajj*. I am a professor at Wellesley College in the *Department of Political Science*, and I am in

Palestinian refugee camps in Lebanon (Jordan) undertaking research that will be used in my research manuscript.

I am studying the formation of property rights and ownership of resources in business sectors in the refugee camps.

The information you share with me will be of great value in helping me complete this research project, the results of which could significantly enhance our understanding of property rights and development.

This interview will take about thirty minutes to one hour of your time.

There is no risk of a breach of confidentiality. I will not link your name to anything you say, either in the transcript of this survey or interview or in the text of my manuscript or any other publications. There are no other expected risks of participation.

Participation is voluntary. If you decide not to participate, there will be no penalty or loss of benefits to which you are otherwise entitled. You can, of course, decline to be interviewed, as well as to stop participating at any time, without any penalty or loss of benefits to which you are otherwise entitled.

If you have any additional questions concerning this research or your participation in it, please feel free to contact me or our college research office at any time."

(The respondent will be given an information card, when applicable, containing name, institutional affiliation, and contact information.)

"Do you have any questions about this research? Do you agree to participate?

If so, let's begin . . ."

INTERVIEW QUESTIONS APPROVED BY IRB (2004 AND 2005)

Standardized Questionnaires for Business Owners, UNRWA officials, Camp Committee and Political Officials, Electricity and Water Officials

QUESTIONS TO ASK BUSINESS/INDUSTRY OWNERS IN PALESTINIAN REFUGEE CAMPS:

MARKET SHOCKS AND SECTOR INFORMATION

1. What type of business or industry are you in and what kind of products do you make here?
2. How many years have you been in business?
3. Could you tell me a brief history of how your business/industry started and how you got to where you are today? In this history, the following subjects are of interest:

   A. What made you think starting a business was a good idea?
   B. Why did you choose to open the type of business you did?
   C. Who else helped you get started?
   D. Who or what has helped you maintain your business?

4. How many other firms are there that do similar or related work?
5. How much do you earn a month or a year with this business?
6. How many employees do you have? How many are full-time or part-time?
7. Where do you get your raw materials or inputs from? How much do they cost a year?
8. How do raw economic materials enter and how do finished products or services enter or exit refugee camps?
9. To what markets do you normally sell your products? Why do you sell products to these specific markets and not others?

MEASUREMENT OF PROPERTY RIGHTS

1. Do you have written documents or contracts that establish the ownership and protection of your goods?
2. Does everyone benefit from the rules of ownership or protection of property, or do only a few people benefit from such rules?

3. If some benefit from rules and others do not, why is that the case?
4. How do you monitor your property? Are there guards, police forces, or recognized people that watch over your property so that people do not try to take it away?
5. If someone breaks rules regarding your ownership of property, like stealing or taking away your property without your permission, how is that person dealt with?
6. Can you sell or lease your property resource or asset (machinery or time for electricity usage)?

ORIGINS OF PROPERTY RIGHTS

1. How did rules about the use and protection of property develop? Could you provide me with a timeline or history of how rules developed?
2. Who initiated the establishment of the protection of property rights? Who might have opposed them? Did some sort of formal or informal judicial institution exist prior to the actual establishment of the protection of property rights? Did UNRWA have anything to do with all this?
3. When did property rights develop? Were huge economic markets available before the rules developed, or did rules develop prior to the realization of a large market of demand?

   A. At the start of your business, did everyone just agree and recognize your business and investment and you never had a problem protecting your property/business?
   B. Was there conscious decision-making about rules, or did rules largely develop without deliberation and discussion?
   C. Did you rely on family networks and relations to ensure that your investment was protected? In other words, does your family or do your friends play a role in ensuring that your investments are protected?
   D. Did rules that were similar to those from your home country develop to protect your property/business/industry so you simply followed historical tradition?

INTERVIEW QUESTIONS APPROVED BY IRB (2007)

Business Owner: Date:
                                             Camp:
Background:

BACKGROUND ON BUSINESS

1. What kind of business do you have?

   A. Carpentry
   B. Cinderblock or tile
   C. Glass
   D. Iron/Steel/Metal works
   E. Other. Please Specify.

2. How many full-time/part-time employees do you have working here?

   A. Full-time
   B. Part-time

3. Where do you get your raw materials?
   Material   Source
   A.
   B.

MARKET SHOCKS

1. When did you open your business?
2. Did you see market opportunity for your business at that particular time?

   A. Yes
   B. No. Please Explain.

MEASUREMENT OF PROPERTY RIGHTS

1. Do you own the land that your business is on?

    A. Yes
    B. No

If no:

    I. Do you rent this shop space?

        a. Yes
        b. No

If yes:

    I. Did you sign a lease or contract for renting the store?

        a. Yes
        b. No

    II. Who do you rent the property from?

        a. Family
        b. Friend or neighbor
        c. Business acquaintance
        d. Other. Please Explain.

2. Do you have written documents or contracts that establish the owner-ship of your property?

    A. Yes
    B. No

If yes:

    I.   Where did you register your property and where are the documents kept?

          a.   With government officials
          b.   With camp officials
          c.   UNRWA
          d.   With religious officials
          e.   Other. Please explain.

    II.   Were lawyers or witnesses present during the signing of contracts?

          a.   Yes
          b.   No

If no:

        i.   Do you have oral agreements?

            a.   Yes
            b.   No

If yes:

        i.   Are oral agreements secure? Explain.

3. Did you have to apply for a government license to open the business?

    A.   Yes
    B.   No

If yes:

I. What steps did you have to go through to establish business ownership?

   Step 1:
   Step 2:
   Step 3:

If no:

I. Did you have to go through any procedures with UNRWA or the popular camp committee to establish business ownership? What were those procedures?

   Step 1:
   Step 2:
   Step 3:

II. Did you just have an oral agreement that established ownership? What assured you that this type of agreement was safe/that the person would not cheat you?

4. If you were to sell your business, what steps would you have to go through?

   Step 1:
   Step 2:
   Step 3:

5. What would you do if you wanted to pass your business/inheritance on to a family member?

   Action 1:
   Action 2:
   Action 3:

6. Do you ever visit an Islamic official or use Islamic law (Shariah) to transfer property?

   A. Yes. Why?
   B. No. Why?

7. Are there guards or police forces that watch over your property so people do not take it away?

   A. Yes
   B. No

If yes:

   I. Who provides the police/guard function?

      a. Government
      b. Local
      c. Hired security forces
      d. Own guards
      e. Other. Please specify.

If no:

   I. Do you have other ways of protecting your property?

      a. Yes
      b. No

If yes:

   i. What other ways?

      a. Community trust (the belief that your neighbors are trust-worthy and would not steal from you)
      b. Other. Please specify.

8. If a person stole or damaged your property, would you go to court?

    A. Yes
    B. No

If yes:

    I. Are the courts effective in your opinion? Please explain.

If no:

    I. How would you deal with someone that stole from you?

        a. Family members would threaten the criminal's family
        b. Would use religious officials
        c. Would go to camp officials (popular camp committee)
        d. Other. Please explain.

From the way you answered the questions I have just asked, it seems that you have a set of rules that establish the ownership of your business. I want to understand a little bit more about how your rules were formed, so I am going to ask you a series of questions that might help me understand.

GOVERNMENTAL INFLUENCE

1. Did the government create the procedures and rules for how you buy, own, or sell your business?

    A. Yes
    B. No

If yes:

    I.   How did you learn about the particular steps you had to follow to buy, own, or sell your business?

        a.   Government agency
        b.   UNRWA
        c.   Camp officials
        d.   Other. Please specify.

    II.   Is the government mainly helpful or a hindrance in your ability to own property?

        a.   Helpful. In what way?
        b.   Hindrance. In what way?

If no:

    I.   Where did the rules come from?

        a.   Islamic Shariah. Please explain.
        b.   On your own. Please explain.
        c.   Other. Please explain and specify.

EFFICIENCY

    1. When you were figuring out how to make property rules, did you look to the government for help?

       A.   Yes
       B.   No

If yes:

    I.   Were they helpful in teaching you about how to form rules?

        a. Yes
        b. No. Why?

If no:

    I.   Did you look to other refugee camps for help?

        a. Yes
        b. No. Why?

2. Did you want to create rules that made it easier to do business over long distances?

    A. Yes. Why?
    B. No. Why?

3. Today, do you mostly do business with people that you know (friends or family) or do you do business with strangers?

    A. People you know (friends/family). Why?
    B. Strangers. Why?

4. Do you think the rules you have to follow primarily work to enhance the success and efficiency of your business?

    A. Yes. Why and how? For example, does having these rules make you feel like your business is more successful than if there were no rules?
    B. No. Why and how?

DISTRIBUTIONAL

1. Did some members of the camp have more say in how property rules were formed in the camp?

   A. Yes
   B. No

   If yes:

   I. Did your age or family name make a difference in terms of having more say in how rules were formed?

      a. Yes. Please explain.
      b. No. Please explain.

2. What is your citizenship status?

   A. Full citizen
   B. Citizen of Palestine
   C. Palestinian from Gaza
   D. Other. Please specify.

3. Does your citizenship status impact your ability to own property?

   A. Yes
   B. No

   If yes:

   I. In what ways does it impact your ability to own property?

      a. Access to government assistance (loans)
      b. Police protection.
      c. Access to courts
      d. Other. Please specify.

If no:

    I.   Why?

4. Are the rules you have to follow to own property the same or different than the rules of those who are not Palestinians?

    A. Same. Why?
    B. Different. Why?

5. Do business owners with full citizenship have it better in the camps than people without full citizenship in terms of controlling the ownership of their business?

    A. Yes. Please explain.
    B. No. Please explain.

6. Did you get a loan to start your business?

    A. Yes
    B. No

If yes:

    I.   Where did you get the loan from?

        a. Bank
        b. Government
        c. UNRWA
        d. Political organization (political party)
        e. Business association
        f. Family member
        g. Other. Please specify.

II. Does your family name make you have more or less power in accessing money for loans, determining rules, or gaining market success?

    a. More power. Why?
    b. Less power. Why?

HISTORICAL

1. In Palestine, before your family came to the refugee camps, did you live in the city or in the countryside?

    A. City
    B. Countryside

2. What did your family do in Palestine? Were you merchants or farmers?

    A. Merchants
    B. Farmers

3. Did you own land in Palestine?

    A. Yes
    B. No

4. Did your family rent land in Palestine?

    A. Yes
    B. No

5. Did you own a business in Palestine?

    A. Yes
    B. No

6. From your family experiences in Palestine, were you familiar with writing contracts or documents for the ownership of land?

    A.   Yes. Explain.

    B.   No. Explain.

UNRWA QUESTIONS (2004, 2005, 2007)

1. What is the legal status of most refugees in this camp? For example, are they citizens or do they benefit from partial citizenship?
2. What is the relationship like between refugees and the host country government? For example, is it cooperative or conflictual?
3. Does UNRWA or the Palestinian refugees own the land on which the refugee camp is constructed?

    A.   Yes.

    B.   No.

If yes:

    I.   Could you tell me more about how UNRWA/Palestinians acquired this land?

If no:

    I.   How are the Palestinians allowed to stay on this land?

    II.   Do Palestinians have the right to use the land inside the camps?

4. Are Palestinian refugees legally permitted to own property *inside* the refugee camps?

    A.   Yes.

    B.   No.

If yes:

    I.   Who regulates the transfer of property within the camps?

If no:

    I.   Why are they not allowed to own property?

5. Does UNRWA have rules that regulate the transfer of property within the camps?

    A.   Yes.
    B.   No.

If no:

    I.   How do Palestinians establish the ownership of property if the government or UNRWA are not involved? For example, do they use community norms or do they use their common religious faith to establish and enforce ownership?

6. I have noticed that there are many businesses in the camps. Are these businesses licensed and registered somewhere?

    A. Yes.
    B. No.

If yes:

    I.   Who regulates the licenses and where are the registers kept?

If no:

    I.   How do Palestinians themselves regulate these businesses (community norms, etc.)?

7. Do you think the current status of property rights ownership in the camp is optimal or do you think certain things could be better? Please explain.

VERSION 1, FEBRUARY 2012

QUESTIONS TO ASK BUSINESS/INDUSTRY OWNERS IN PALESTINIAN REFUGEE CAMPS:

BACKGROUND

1. What type of business or industry are you in and what kind of products do you make here?
2. How many years have you been in business?
3. Could you tell me a brief history of how your business/industry started and how you got to where you are today? In this history, the following subject areas are of interest:

    A. What made you think starting a business was a good idea?
    B. Why did you choose to open the type of business you did?
    C. Who else helped you get started?
    D. Who or what has helped you maintain your business?

4. How many other firms are there that do similar or related work?
5. How much do you earn a month or a year with this business?
6. How many employees do you have? How many are full-time or part-time?
7. Where do you get your raw materials or inputs from? How much do they cost a year?
8. Since Nahr al-Bared was destroyed in 2007, what has happened to your business?
9. Did UNRWA offer compensation for the loss of your business?
10. Do you have plans to rebuild your business? Why or why not?

MEASUREMENT OF PROPERTY RIGHTS

1. Do you have written documents or contracts that establish the ownership and protection of your business/home?
2. Does everyone benefit from the rules of ownership or protection of property, or do only a few people benefit from such rules?
3. If some benefit from rules and others do not, why is that the case?
4. How do you monitor your property? Are there guards, police forces, or recognized people that watch over your property so that people do not try to take it away?
5. If someone breaks rules regarding your ownership of property, like stealing or taking away your property without your permission, how is that person dealt with?
6. Can you sell or lease your property resource or asset (machinery or time for electricity usage)?

ORIGINS OF PROPERTY RIGHTS

1. How did rules about the use and protection of property develop? Could you provide me with a timeline or history of how rules developed?
2. Who initiated the establishment of the protection of property rights? Who might have opposed them? Did some sort of formal or informal judicial institution exist prior to the actual establishment of the protection of property rights? Did UNRWA have anything to do with all this?
3. When did property rights develop? Were huge economic markets available before the rules developed, or did rules develop prior to the realization of a large market of demand?

    A. At the start of your business, did everyone just agree and recognize your business and investment and you never had a problem protecting your property/business?
    B. Was there conscious decision making about rules, or did they largely develop without deliberation and discussion?

C. Did you rely on family networks and relations to ensure that your investment was protected? In other words, does your family or do your friends play a role in ensuring that your investments are protected?

D. Did rules that were similar to rules from your home country develop to protect your property/business/industry so you simply followed historical tradition?

النسخه الاولى فبراير

2012

أسئلة لأصحاب المشاريع التجارية او الصناعية في مخيمات اللاجئين الفلسطينيين .

خلفية الموضوع

1 ما هي نوع التجارة او الصناعة التي تمارسها؟ ما هي نوع المنتجات التي تصنعها؟

2 كم سنه وانت تمارس هذا العمل؟

3 هل من الممكن ان تكتب موجز عن بداية مشروعك التجاري او الصناعي وكيف وصلت الى المكانة التي انت فيها الان؟حين تجيب عن هذا السؤال ارجوا ان تتحدث عن المواضيع التالية بالتفصيل :-

- ما الذي جعلك تتصور ان اقامه مشروعك التجاري فكرة جيدة؟

- لماذا اخترت ان تمارس هذا النوع من التجارة ؟

- من ساعدك في انشاء هذا العمل؟

- من وما الذي ساعدك على المحافظة على عملك؟

4 كم عدد المشاريع او الشركات الاخرى التي تقوم بنفس عملك او عملا يشابه عملك؟

5 كم تكسب شهريا او سنويا من هذا العمل؟

6 كم عدد عمالك او موظفيك ؟ كم منهم يعمل دوام كامل وكم منهم يعمل نصف دوام؟

7 من اين تحصل على المواد الاولية او الخام؟ كم تكلفك هذه المواد في السنة؟

8 منذ ان تدمر مخيم نهر البارد في 2007, ماذا حدث لتجارتك؟

9 هل قدمت لك منظمة الاونروا اي تعويضات لفقدان تجارتك؟

10 هل تخطط على اعادة بناء مشروعك؟ لماذا نعم او لا؟

قياس حقوق الملكية

1 هل لديك او اوراق مكتوبة او عقود تؤكد الملكية وتحمي منزلك او تجارتك؟

2 هل يستفاد الكل من قوانين الملكية او حمايه الملكية ام يستفاد فقط القليل من الناس من هذه القوانين؟

3 اذا كان البعض يستفاد من هذه القوانين والأخرون لا يستفادون, فما هو السبب ؟

4 كيف تحمي ملكك؟ هل هناك حراس او قوات شرطة او اشخاص معينين يراقبون الاملاك ويحرسوها حتى لا يستطيع احد من الناس ان يستولي على املاك الاخرين؟

5 في حاله مخالفه قوانين الملكيه وقام احد بالاسيلاء على ملكك وسرقته كيف يتم التعامل مع هذا الشخص؟

6 هل تستطيع ان تبيع او تأجر المعدات او المكائن التي تملكها وهل تستطيع ان تبيع او تؤجر الحصة الممنوحه لك ممن الطاقة الكهربائية؟

اصول حقوق الملكية

كيف بدأت وتطورت قوانين استخدام وحماية الملكية؟ هل من الممكن ان تعطي جدول زمني او تاريخ عن كيفيه تطور القوانين ؟

1 من بدأ تاسيس حماية الحقوق الملكية ؟ من من المحتمل ان يكون عارض تاسيس حماية حقوق الملكية ؟ هل كانت هناك مؤسسات قضائية رسمية وغير رسمية موجودة قبل انشاء حماية حقوق الملكية ؟ هل كان لمنظمة الاونروا دور في الموضوع؟

2 متى تطورت قوانين حماية الملكية؟ هل تطورت من خلال وجود تعاملات تجارية وسوق كبير ؟ ام ان القوانين اصلا موجودة قبل نمو التجارة والطلب والاسواق ؟

مثلا, هل بدأت مشروعك التجاري والكل وافقوا واعترفوا بمشروعك واستثمارك التجاري ولم يكن لديك اي مشكلة بحماية ملكك او تجارتك؟

هل كان هناك قرار واعي بضرورة أنشاء القوانين ام نشأت من دون مناقشة وتدبير؟

هل كنت ضمن شبكة معارف وعلاقات لحماية عملك؟ بعبارة اخرى هل هناك دور للمعارف والعائلة والاقارب في حماية العمل والاستثمارات؟

ام ان القوانين المتبعة لحماية الحقوق الملكية مشابهة لقوانين الوطن الام وانتم قمتم باتباعها كعرف تقليدي؟

UNRWA NAHR AL-BARED REBUILD INFORMATION: 2007 AND NAHR AL-BARED RECONSTRUCTION

1. Could you please explain to me the condition of Nahr al-Bared shortly after the 2007 conflict? For example, was the entire camp destroyed or was there a portion left intact? Was the plumbing and electrical infrastructure intact?

2. After the 2007 conflict, how did UNRWA deal with residents of Nahr al-Bared that lost their homes?

3. After the 2007 conflict, how did UNRWA deal with residents of Nahr al-Bared that lost their businesses?

4. How was compensation determined?

5. Who determined levels of compensation?

6. Did UNRWA deal with any political groups/business people/camp elders in the camps when negotiating the compensation?

7. How were Nahr al-Bared refugees resettled after the 2007 conflict?

8. How did Beddawi change as a result of the influx of Nahr al-Bared refugees?

9. Has there been a change in the number of businesses in Nahr al-Bared?

10. Who was involved in the decision to rebuild Nahr al-Bared?

11. Who is involved in rebuilding Nahr al-Bared?

12. What is the timeline for rebuilding Nahr al-Bared?

13. How will the new Nahr al-Bared differ from the old Nahr al-Bared?

    A. In appearance:

    B. In regulations for businesses and development:

    C. In residents (number and profile):

STATUS OF THE "NEW" NAHR AL-BARED

1. Does UNRWA own the land on which Nahr al-Bared is constructed today?

    A. Yes.

    B. No.

If yes:

    I. Could you tell me more about how UNRWA/Palestinians acquired this land?

If no:

    I. How are the Palestinians allowed to stay on this land?

    II. Do Palestinians have the right to use the land inside the camps (usufructuary rights)?

2. Are Palestinian refugees legally permitted to own property *inside* the new Nahr al-Bared?

    A.   Yes.

    B.   No.

If yes:

    I. Who regulates the transfer of property within the camps?

If no:

    I.   Why are they not allowed to own property?

3. Does UNRWA have rules that regulate the transfer of property within the new Nahr al-Bared camp?

    A.   Yes.

    B.   No.

If no:

I. How do Palestinians establish ownership of property if the government or UNRWA are not involved? For example, do they use community norms or their common religious faith to establish and enforce ownership?

معلومات الاونروا عن اعادة بناء نهر البارد

واعادة اعمار نهر البارد 2007

1. هل من الممكن ان تشرح لي حالة نهر البارد بعد خلاف عام ٢٠٠٧؟ مثلا هل دمر المخيم كله ام بقيهت هناك اجزاء لم تدمر وسليمة ؟ هل سلمت انابيب المياه والبنية التحتية الكهربائية؟

٢. بعد خلاف ٢٠٠٧, كيف تعاملت منظمة الاونروا مع سكان نهر البارد الذين قد فقدوا منازلهم؟

٣. بعد خلاف ٢٠٠٧, كيف تعاملت منظمة الاونروا مع سكان نهر البارد الذين قد فقدوا تجارتهم؟

٤. كيف حددت التعويضات؟

٥. من حدد درجات التعويض؟

٦.هل تعاملت الاونروا مع اي مجموعات سياسية, أو رجال اعمال, أو كبار المخيم في المخيمات حين تفاوضوا عن التعويضات؟

٧.كيف اعيد اسكان لاجئين نهر البارد بعد أزمة ٢٠٠٧؟

٨.كيف تغيرت بدوي بسبب تدفق اللاجئين من نهر البارد؟

٩. هل تغير عدد المشاريع التجارية في نهر البارد؟

١٠. من شارك في قرار اعادة بناء نهر البارد؟

١١. ما هي المدة الزمنية المحددة لبناء نهر البارد؟

١٢. كيف سيكون نهر البارد الجديد مختلفا عن نهر البارد القديم؟

في المظهر

في القوانين عن التجارة والتنمية

في عدد ونوع السكان

حالة نهر البارد الجديد

١. هل تملك الاونروا الارض التي مشيد عليها نهر البارد اليوم؟

اذا كان الجواب نعم, هل لك أن تخبرني كيف حصلت الاونروا او الفسطينون على هذه الارض؟

اذا كان الجواب لا , فكيف سمح للفلسطنين في البقاء على هذه الارض؟

اذا كان الجواب لا, فهل للفلسطينين الحق في أستخدام الارض داخل المخيمات (الحقوق الانتفاعية) ؟

٢. هل مسموح قانونيا لللاجئين الفلسطينين بأن يملكوا ارض داخل نهر البارد الجديد؟

اذا كان الجواب نعم, فمن يدير نقل الملكية داخل المخيمات؟

اذا كان الجواب لا, فلماذا ليس مسموح لهم بأمتلاك الممتلكات.

٣. هل لدى اونروا قوانين تنضم نقل الملكية داخل مخيم نهر البارد الجديد؟

اذا كان الجواب لا, فكيف يستطبع الفلسطينيون أمتلاك ملك اذا كانت الحكومة والاونروا غير متدخلين في الموضوع؟ مثلا, هل يستخدمون أعراف المجتمع أو أعتقادهم الديني الشائع لكي يأسسوا وينفذوا الملكية؟

NOTES

INTRODUCTION

1. A complete list of interview respondents can be found in appendix B.

1. A THEORY OF PROPERTY RIGHTS FORMATION IN PALESTINIAN REFUGEE CAMPS

1. Charles Smith, "World War II and the Creation of the State of Israel," in *Palestine and the Arab-Israeli Conflict: A History with Documents* (New York: St. Martin's Press, 2010), 165–221.
2. Avi Shlaim, "The Debate About 1948," *International Journal of Middle East Studies* 27, no. 3 (August 1995): 287–302, provides a concise outline of the different perspectives on 1948. It is worth further consideration for readers interested in the question.
3. For more reading, see Alexander Gerschenkron, *Economic Backwardness in Historical Perspective* (Cambridge, Mass.: Harvard University Press, 1962); S. Markus, "Secure Property as a Bottom-Up Process: Firms, Stakeholders, and Predators in Weak States," *World Politics* 64, no. 2 (2012): 242–77; Y. Qian, "How Reform Worked in China," in *In Search of Prosperity*, ed. D. Rodrik (Princeton, N.J.: Princeton University Press, 2003); Andrei Shleifer, *Without a Map* (Cambridge, Mass.: MIT Press, 2001); Kathleen Thelen,

"Historical Institutionalism in Comparative Politics," *Annual Review of Political Science* 2 (June 1999): 369–404; Kathleen Thelen, *How Institutions Evolve* (Cambridge, Mass.: Cambridge University Press, 2004).

4. For more background, see Lee Alston, Gary Libecap, and Bernardo Mueller, *Titles, Conflict, and Land Use: The Development of Property Rights and Land Reform on the Brazilian Amazon Frontier* (Ann Arbor: University of Michigan Press, 1999); Abhijit Banarjee and Esther Duflo, *Poor Economics: A Radical Rethinking of the Way to Fight Global Poverty* (Cambridge, Mass.: Public Affairs, 2011); Robert Ellickson, "A Hypothesis of Wealth–Maximizing Norms: Evidence from the Whaling Industry," *Journal of Law, Economics, and Organization* 5 (1989): 83–97; Jean Ensminger, "Changing Property Rights: Reconciling Formal and Information Right to Land in Africa," in *The Frontiers of the New Institutional Economics*, ed. Drobak and Ny (San Diego, Calif.: Academic Press, 1997), 165–96; Elinor Ostrom, *Governing the Commons: The Evolution of Institutions for Collective Action* (Cambridge, Mass.: Cambridge University Press, 1990).

5. For clarification, see John Harriss, Janet Hunter, and Colin Lewis, "Introduction: Development and Significance of NIE," in *The New Institutional Economics and Third World Development* (New York: Routledge, 1995), 1–16; Jack Knight, *Institutions and Social Conflict* (Cambridge, Mass.: Cambridge University Press, 1992); Douglass North and Robert Thomas, *The Rise of the Western World: A New Economic History* (Cambridge, Mass.: Cambridge University Press, 1973); Douglass C. North, "The New Institutional Economics and Third World Development," in *The New Institutional Economics and Third World Development*, ed. John Harriss, Janet Hunter, and Colin Lewis (New York: Routledge, 1995), 7–26; Douglass North and Barry R. Weingast, "Constitutions and Commitment: The Evolution of Institutions Governing Public Choice in Seventeenth-Century England," *Journal of Economic History* 49 (December 1989): 803–32.

6. Golda Meir, the fourth prime minister of Israel in March 1969, said in the *Sunday Times* on June 15, 1969, that the Palestinian people did not exist and that the newspaper could publish her words without the slightest qualm:

> There were no such thing as Palestinians. When was there an independent Palestinian people with a Palestinian state? It was either southern Syria before the First World War, and then it was a Palestine including Jordan. It was not as though there was a Palestinian people in Palestine considering itself as a Palestinian people and we came and threw them out and took their country away from them. They did not exist. (*Sunday Times*, June 15, 1969; *Washington Post*, June 16, 1969)

7. Article 3 of the 1954 law states that a Jordanian national is "any person with previous Palestinian nationality except the Jews before the date of May 15, 1948 residing in the Kingdom during the period from December 20, 1949 and February 16, 1954." It is important to highlight that the announcement of formal privileges to property rights for Palestinians did not mean that formal property rights had formed or were present inside the refugee camps at that time. It was not until the departure of Fatah in 1969/1970 that formal property rights formed inside refugee camps in Jordan.

8. Current West Bank residents that live there on a full-time basis no longer hold Jordanian nationality because they are now under the jurisdiction of the Palestinian Authority. Therefore Palestinians that live permanently in the West Bank can now apply for a temporary Jordanian passport and can visit Jordan only on a temporary basis for work, education, or vacation (See el-Abed, Oroub, "Immobile Palestinians: The impact of policies and practices on Palestinians from Gaza in Jordan," in *France Migrants et Migrations au Moyen-Orient au tournant du XXIe siècle*, ed. Jaber, Hana, and Metral [Beyrouth: Institut Français du Proche Orient, 2005], 81–93). They must apply for a work permit and for the right to own property from the ministerial council.

9. Notably, the chart has been adapted from el-Abed's (2005) research and charts.

10. This percentage is based on interviews with refugee businessmen and officials during my 2007 interviews in Jordan. The list of individuals I interviewed is located in appendix B. The exact percentage of Gazans in each camp is unknown; nevertheless, the percentage reveals that the population in Baqa'a has refugees with varying citizenship backgrounds.

2. CRAFTING INFORMAL PROPERTY RIGHTS IN *FAWDAH*

1. Notably, Sayigh and Knudsen translate *tawtin*, derived from the root word *watan*, or nation, to mean implantation or integration. See Rosemary Sayigh, "Palestinians in Lebanon: Harsh Present, Uncertain Future," *Journal of Palestine Studies* 25 (1995): 37–53; and, Are Knudsen, "Widening the Protection Gap: The 'Politics of Citizenship' for Palestinian Refugees in Lebanon, 1948–2008," *Journal of Refugee Studies* 22, no. 1 (1995): 51–73.

2. Though some families moved outside of the camps, Palestinians were not legally allowed to own land, a home, or a business in their name in land located outside of the refugee camps. This was especially the case in Lebanon. In Jordan, Palestinians that were not of 1967 Gazan descent could move outside the camps and theoretically own property, but for most it was an unlikely prospect because the cost of owning a house or a business outside the camps was prohibitively expensive during the early decades there.

3. FORMAL PROPERTY RIGHTS IN REFUGEE CAMPS IN JORDAN

1. It is unclear if community leaders inside the camps had strong connections with Palestinian political groups. It is possible that many community leaders maintained connections with political groups, though I suspect that if those linkages existed they remained secretive given the political climate. Future research in the camps should explore the historical linkages between community/tribal leaders and Palestinian political parties and the influence this had on the goals and strategies of community leaders during negotiations with Jordanian officials.

4. FORMAL PROPERTY RIGHTS IN REFUGEE CAMPS IN LEBANON

1. Arafat and many Fatah-PLO followers were self-described centrist nationalists and were relatively indifferent to class struggle and Marxism-Leninism. They were still considered radical because they positioned themselves against Arab theorizing. "We do not have ideology—our goal is the liberation of our fatherland by any means necessary . . . by blood and iron." In the interview, Arafat was defending Fatah's decision to accept funding from Arab countries regardless of their political orientation, whether they were right, center, or left in ideological bent. See B. Rubin, *The PLO Under Arafat* (New Haven, Conn.: Yale University Press, 1994), 19.

2. Sura 4:19 in the Quran says: "O you who believe! You are forbidden to inherit women against their will, and you should not treat them with harshness that you may take back part of the [Mahr] dower you have given them."

3. UNRWA and the electricity company played a role in establishing the infrastructure of resource delivery, but they were not a part of the property rights negotiations. UNRWA held an explicit policy of not interfering with the formation of property rights and the Cairo Accords limited the access of Lebanese political groups (as well as Lebanese companies) in the camps. The electricity company could not participate in the camps' institutional negotiations.

5. RENEGOTIATING PROPERTY RIGHTS IN NAHR AL-BARED CAMP

1. Another indicator that Fatah al-Islam was from outside the camp was reflected in the strategy the group used to gain a foothold in the local NBC

population. In order to claim some connection to the local Palestinians, they encouraged conscripts to marry women from NBC. Many women in Nahr al-Bared refugee camp felt disgusted by the marriage matches with Fatah al-Islam. "The only families that let their daughters marry these guys were very poor and destitute. They were doing it for the money. We all knew these men would be dead and become martyrs in the next few months. Clearly, they would not win their battles. The NBC girls will get money for marrying the guys and, with any luck, wouldn't be able to conceive children so quickly. Fatah al-Islam wants to encourage the weddings so they can say they are 'men from the camps that have married into the old families and villages of Nahr al-Bared.' These poor women have no choice" (I-57L).

REFERENCES

Abouzeid, Rania. 2003. "No Property Rights for Lebanon's Refugees." October 30. http://english.aljazeera.net/NR/exeres/9DC5B37F-A3FB-4781-9642 -0126711DA4A7.htm (October 20, 2004).

Acemoglu, Daron, et al. 2003. "An African Success Story: Botswana." In *In Search of Prosperity*, ed. Dani Rodrik, 80–119. Princeton, N.J.: Princeton University Press.

Acheson, James. 1988. *Lobster Gangs of Maine.* Hanover, NH: University Press of New England.

Allio, Lorene, et al. 1997. "Post-Communist Privatization as a Test of Theories of Institutional Change." In *The Political Economy of Property Rights*, ed. David L. Weimer, 319–349. New York: Cambridge University Press.

Alston, Lee. 2005. "The 'Case' for Case Studies in Political Economy." *The Political Economist* 12 (Spring–Summer): 1, 8, 10, 14–19.

Alston, Lee, Gary Libecap, and Bernardo Mueller. 1999. *Titles, Conflict, and Land Use: The Development of Property Rights and Land Reform on the Brazilian Amazon Frontier.* Ann Arbor: University of Michigan Press.

Anderson, Lisa, et al. 2007. "Comparative Politics of the Middle East and Academic Freedom." *APSA-CP Newsletter* 18 (1): 12–15.

Anderson, Terry, and Peter Hill. 2004. *The Not so Wild, Wild West: Property Rights on the Frontier.* Stanford: Stanford University Press.

Anderson, Terry, and Laura Huggins. 2003. *Property Rights.* Stanford: Hoover Press.

Armanazi, Ghayth. 1974. "The Rights of the Palestinians: The International Definition." *Journal of Palestine Studies* 3 (Spring): 88–96.

Axelrod, Robert. 1984. *The Evolution of Cooperation*. Cambridge, Mass.: Basic Books.

Banarjee, Abhijit, and Esther Duflo. 2011. *Poor Economics: A Radical Rethinking of the Way to Fight Global Poverty*. Cambridge, Mass.: Public Affairs.

Barzel, Yoram. 1997. *Economic Analysis of Property Rights*. Cambridge, Mass.: Cambridge University Press.

Bates, Robert. 2004. "On The Politics of Property Rights by Haber, Razo, and Maurer." *Journal of Economic Literature* 42 (June): 494–500.

Baum, Matthew, and David Lake. 2003. "The Political Economy of Growth: Democracy and Human Capital." *American Journal of Political Science* 47 (April): 333–47.

Bellesiles, Michael. 1993. *Revolutionary Outlaws: Ethan Allen and the Struggle for Independence on the Early American Frontier*. Charlottesville, Va.: University of Virginia Press.

Bennett, Andrew, and Alexander L. George. 2004. *Case Studies and Theory Development in the Social Sciences*. Cambridge, Mass.: MIT Press.

Besley, Timothy. 1995. "Property Rights and Investment Incentives: Theory and Evidence from Ghana." *The Journal of Political Economy* 104 (October): 903–937.

Brand, Laurie. 1988. *Palestinians in the Arab World*. New York: Columbia University Press.

Butters, Andrew Lee. 2008. "The Ruins of Nahr al-Bared." March 14. http://time-blog.com/middle_east/2008/03/nahr_albared_was_once_one.html?xid=rss-mideast (March 14, 2008).

Cammett, Melani. 2007. "The War on Terror: Implications for Research and Data Collection in the Middle East." *APSA-CP Newsletter* (Winter): 16–19.

Chang, Ha Joon. 2000. "Institutional Development in Developing Countries in a Historical Perspective—Lessons from Developed Countries in Earlier Times." Presented at the European Association of Evolutionary Political Economy, Siena. http://www.networkideas.org/featart/mar2002/Institutional_Development.pdf (March 18, 2004).

Checkel, Jeffrey. 2005. "International Institutions and Socialization in Europe: Introduction and Framework." *International Organization*. Special issue.

Christoff, Stefan. 2004. "Living War: Palestinian Refugees in Lebanon." January 14. http://www.zmag.org/content/print_article.cfm?itemID=4837&sectionID=22 (October 20, 2004).

Coase, Robert H. 1960. "The Problem of Social Cost." *The Journal of Law and Economics* 3 (October): 1–44.

Copes, Parzival. 1986. "A Critical Review of the Individual Quota as a Device in Fisheries Management." *Local Economics* 62 (August): 278–91.

Curzon, George. 1907. *Frontiers*. Oxford: Clarendon Press.

Dann, Uriel. 1989. *King Hussein and the Challenge of Arab Radicalism*. New York: Oxford University Press.

de Lavaleye, Emile. 1878. *Primitive Property*. Trans. G. R. L. Marriott. London: Macmillan.

De Soto, H. 1989. *The Other Path: The Invisible Revolution in the Third World*. New York: Harper and Row.

Demsetz, Harold. 1967. "Toward a Theory of Property Rights." *The American Economic Review* 57 (2): 347–59.

Divine, Donna. 1994. *Politics and Society in Ottoman Palestine: The Arab Struggle for Survival and Power*. Boulder, Colo.: Lynne Reiner.

Doumani, Beshara. 1995. *Rediscovering Palestine: Merchants and Peasants in Jabal Nablus, 1700–1900*. Berkeley: University of California Press.

el-Abed, Oroub. 2005. "Immobile Palestinians: The impact of policies and practices on Palestinians from Gaza in Jordan," in *France Migrants et Migrations au Moyen-Orient au tournant du XXIe siècle*, Jaber, Hana, and Metral, 81–93. Beyrouth : Institut Français du Proche Orient.

Ellickson, Robert. 1989. "A Hypothesis of Wealth—Maximizing Norms: Evidence from the Whaling Industry." *Journal of Law, Economics, and Organization* 5: 83–97.

Elster, Jon. 1989. "Social Norms and Economic Theory." *The Journal of Economic Perspectives* 3 (4): 99–117.

Ensminger, Jean. 1992. *Making a Market: The Institutional Transformation of an African Society*. Cambridge, Mass.: Cambridge University Press.

——. 1997. "Changing Property Rights: Reconciling Formal and Information Right to Land in Africa." In *The Frontiers of the New Institutional Economics*, ed. John Drobak and John Nye, 165–96. San Diego, Calif.: Academic Press.

Evans, Peter. 1995. *Embedded Autonomy: States and Industrial Transformation*. Princeton, N.J.: Princeton University Press.

Farsoun, Samih, and Christina Zacharia. 1997. *Palestine and the Palestinians*. Boulder, Colo.: Westview Press.

Feldman, Ilana. 2008. *Governing Gaza: Bureaucracy, Authority, and the Work of Rule, 1917–1967*. Durham, N.C.: Duke University Press.

Fenno, R. 1986. "Observation, Context, and Sequence in the Study of Politics." *American Political Science Review* 80 (1): 3–15.

Fischbach, Michael. 2003. *Records of Dispossession: Palestinian Refugee Property and the Arab-Israeli Conflict*. New York: Columbia University Press.

Frye, Timothy. 1999. "The Politics of Post- Communist Economic Reform." Transition Report. European Bank for Reconstruction and Development. London.

——. 2000. *Brokers and Bureaucrats: Building Market Institutions in Russia*. Ann Arbor: University of Michigan Press.

Galiani, Sebastian, and Ernesto Schargrodsky. 2010. "Property Rights for the Poor: Effects of Land Titling." *Journal of Public Economics* 94 (October): 700–729.

Geertz, Clifford. 1963. *Peddlers and Princes: Social Change and Economic Modernization in Two Indonesian Towns*. Chicago: University of Chicago Press.

Gerber, Haim. 1994. *The Social Origins of the Modern Middle East*. Boulder, Colo.: Lynne Reiner.

Gerschenkron, Alexander. 1962. *Economic Backwardness in Historical Perspective*. Cambridge, Mass.: Harvard University Press.

Graeber, David. 2004. *Fragments of an Anarchist Anthropology*. Chicago: Prickly Paradigm Press.

Grindle, Merilee. 2001. "In Quest of the Political: The Political Economy of Development Policymaking." In *Frontiers of Development Economics*, ed. Gerald M. Meier and Joseph E. Stiglitz, 344–75. Oxford: Oxford University Press.

Gubser, Peter. 1983. *Jordan: Crossroads of Middle Eastern Events*. Boulder, Colo.: Westview Press.

Haber, Stephen, Douglass C. North, and Barry R. Weingast. 2002. "The Poverty Trap." *Hoover Digest*, Fall. http:///www.hooverdigest.org/024/haber.html (November 8, 2004).

Hajj, Nadya. 2014. "Institutional Formation in Transitional Settings." *The Journal of Comparative Politics* 46 (4): 399–418.

Hall, Peter A., and Rosemary Taylor. 1996. "Political Science and the Three New Institutionalisms." *Political Studies* 44 (December): 936–58.

Hamid, Rashid. 1975. "What Is the PLO?" *Journal of Palestine Studies* 4 (4): 90–109.

Hanafi, Sair, and T. Long. 2010. "Governance, Governmentalities, and the State of Exception in the Palestinian Refugee Camps of Lebanon." *Journal of Refugee Studies* 23 (2): 134–59.

Hanafi, Sari, and Are Knudsen. 2010a. "Governing the Palestinian Refugee Camps in Lebanon and Syria." In *Palestinian Refugees: Identity, Space, and Place in the Levant*, 29–49. New York: Taylor and Francis.

——. 2010b. "Nahr al Bared: The Political Fallout of a Refugee Disaster." In *Palestinian Refugees: Identity, Space, and Place in the Levant*, 97–110. New York: Taylor and Francis.

Harriss, John. 2006. "Notes on a Historical Institutional Approach to the IPPG Agenda." University of Manchester. Typescript. http://www.dfid.gov.uk/r4d/PDF/Outputs/ProPoor_RPC/IPPGDP1.pdf (November 4, 2012).

Harriss, John, Janet Hunter, and Colin Lewis. 1995. "Introduction: Development and Significance of NIE." In *The New Institutional Economics and Third World Development*, ed. John Harriss et al., 1–16. New York: Routledge.

Hay, Colin, and Daniel Wincott. 1998. "Structure, Agency and Historical Institutionalism." *Political Studies* 46 (December): 951–57.

Heller, Patrick. 1999. *The Labor of Development: Workers and the Transformation of Capitalism in Kerala, India*. Ithaca, N.Y.: Cornell University Press.

Helliwell, J. 1994. "Empirical Linkages Between Democracy and Economic Growth." *British Journal of Political Science* 24 (2): 225–48.

Hess, Charlotte, and Sandra F. Joireman. 2007. "Enforcing New Property Rights in Sub-Saharan Africa: The Ugandan Constitution and the 1998 Land Act." *Comparative Politics* 39 (July): 463–80.

Jacobsen, Karen. 2005. *The Economic Life of Refugees*. Bloomfield, Conn.: Kumarian Press.

Jordan, Grant. 1990. "Policy Community Realism versus 'New' Institutionalist Ambiguity." *Political Studies* 38 (September): 470–84.

Kagan, Michael. 2009. "The (Relative) Decline of Palestinian Exceptionalism and Its Consequences for Refugee Studies in the Middle East." *Journal of Refugee Studies* 22 (4): 417–38.

Kanafani, Ghassan. 1999. *Men in the Sun*. Boulder, Colo.: Lynne Rienner English Translation.

Katznelson, Ira, and Barry R. Weingast. 2005. "Intersections Between Historical and Rational Choice Institutionalism." In *Preferences and Situations: Points of Intersection Between Historical and Rational Choice Institutionalism*, ed. Ira Katznelson and Barry R. Weingast, 1–24. New York: Russell Sage Foundation.

Keefer, Phillip. 2005. "From Settler Mortality to Patrimonialism: Weaving the Dynamics of Political Competition into the Political Economy of Development." *The Political Economist* 12 (Winter): 1, 5, 8, 10, 13.

Kemal, Lorenzo. 2014. "Whose Land? Land Tenure in late Nineteenth- and Early Twentieth-Century Palestine." *British Journal of Middle Eastern Studies* 41 (2): 230–42.

Khalidi, Rashid. 1988. *Palestinian Identity: The Construction of Modern National Consciousness*. New York: Columbia University Press.

King, Gary, et al. 1994. *Designing Social Inquiry*. Princeton, N.J.: Princeton University Press.

Knight, Jack. 1992. *Institutions and Social Conflict*. Cambridge, Mass.: Cambridge University Press.

Knudsen, Are. 2009. "Widening the Protection Gap: The 'Politics of Citizenship' for Palestinian Refugees in Lebanon, 1948–2008." *Journal of Refugee Studies* 22 (1): 51–73.

Lane, Frederic. 1979. *Power from Profits: Readings in Protection Rent and Violence-Controlling Enterprises*. Albany: State University of New York Press.

Layish, Aharon. 2008. "Islamization of Custom as Reflected in Awards of Tribal Arbitrators in the Judean Desert." *Jerusalem Studies in Arabic and Islam* 35 (May): 285–334.

Leblang, D. 1994. "Property Rights, Democracy and Economic Growth." Thomas Jefferson Program in Public Policy Working Paper No. 27. College of William and Mary.

Libecap, Gary D. 1989. *Contracting for Property Rights.* Cambridge, Mass.: Cambridge University Press.

Lijphart, Arend. 1971. "Comparative Politics and the Comparative Method." *The American Political Science Review* 65 (September): 682–93.

Lindsay, A. D. 1913. "The Principle of Private Property." In *Property: Its Duties and Rights, Historically, Philosophically and Religiously Regarded,* ed. Charles Gore and Leonard Trelawny Hobhouse, 65–81. London: Macmillan.

Mair, Johanna, and Ignasi Marti. 2009. "Entrepreneurship in and around Institutional Voids: A Case Study from Bangladesh." *Journal of Business Venturing.* 24 (5): 419–435.

Mansuri, Ghazala, and Vijayendra Rao. 2012. *Localizing Development: Does Participation Work?* Washington, D.C.: World Bank Publications.

March, J., and J. Olsen. 1984. "The New Institutionalism: Organizational Factors in Political Life." *American Political Science Review* 78 (3): 734–49.

——. 2005. "Elaborating the 'New Institutionalism.'" University of Oslo. Typescript. http://www.cpp.amu.edu.pl/pdf/olsen2.pdf (March 2005).

Markus, S. 2012. "Secure Property as a Bottom-Up Process: Firms, Stakeholders, and Predators in Weak States." *World Politics* 64 (2): 242–77.

Maxfield, Sylvia, and Ben Ross Schneider. 1997. *Business and the State in Developing Countries.* Ithaca, N.Y.: Cornell University Press.

Montinola, Gabriella, Yingyi Quan, and Barry R. Weingast. 1995. "Federalism Chinese Style: The Political Basis for Economic Success in China." *World Politics* 48 (October): 50–81.

Moravcsik, Andy. 2010. "Active Citation: A Precondition for Replicable Qualitative Research." *PS: Political Science and Politics* 43 (1): 29–35.

Nadan, Amos. 2006. *The Palestinian Peasant Economy under the Mandate: A Story of Colonial Bungling.* Cambridge, Mass.: Harvard University Press.

North, Douglass C. 1995. "The New Institutional Economics and Third World Development." In *The New Institutional Economics and Third World Development,* ed. John Harriss et al., 17–26. New York: Routledge.

North, Douglass, and Robert Thomas. 1973. *The Rise of the Western World: A New Economic History.* Cambridge, Mass.: Cambridge University Press.

North, Douglass, and Barry R. Weingast. 1989. "Constitutions and Commitment: The Evolution of Institutions Governing Public Choice in Seventeenth-Century England." *The Journal of Economic History* 49 (December): 803–32.

Nunn, Nathan. 2008. "The Long-Term Effects of Africa's Slave Trade." *Quarterly Journal of Economics* (February): 139–76.

Olson, M. 1993. "Dictatorship, Democracy, and Development." *American Political Science Review* 87 (3): 567–76.

———. 2000. *Power and Prosperity: Outgrowing Communist and Capitalist Dictatorships.* New York: Basic Books.

Ostrom, Elinor. 1990. *Governing the Commons: The Evolution of Institutions for Collective Action.* Cambridge, Mass.: Cambridge University Press.

———. 2000. "Private and Common Property Rights." *Encyclopedia of Law and Economics.* Vol. II: *Civil Law and Economics:* 332–79.

Ostrom, Elinor, and Schlager. 1992. "Property Right Regimes and Natural Resources." *Land Economics* 68 (3): 249–62.

Ostrom, Elinor, et al. 1994. *Rules, Games, and Common Pool Resources.* Ann Arbor: University of Michigan Press.

Peteet, Julie M. 1997. "Lebanon: Palestinian Refugees in the Post-War Period." *Le Monde Diplomatique*, December HCR Report (19).

Peters, B. G. 1999. *Institutional Theory in Political Science: The "New" Institutionalism.* London: Pinter.

Pierson, Paul. 2000. "Not Just What, but When: Timing and Sequence in Political Process." *American Political Development* 14: 72–92.

———. 2004. *Politics in Time: History, Institutions, and Social Analysis.* Princeton, N.J. Princeton University Press.

Prescott, J.R.V. 1987. *Political Frontiers and Boundaries.* London: Unwin Hyman.

Qian, Y. 2003. "How Reform Worked in China." In *In Search of Prosperity*, ed. D. Rodrik, 297–333. Princeton, N.J.: Princeton University Press.

Ragin, Charles C. 1987. *The Comparative Method: Moving Beyond Qualitative and Quantitative Strategies.* Berkeley: University of California Press.

Riker, W., and Ital Sened. 1991. "A Political Theory of the Origin of Property Rights: Airport Slots." *American Journal of Political Science* 35 (4): 951–69.

Roberts, Rebecca. 2010. *The Palestinians in Lebanon.* London: I. B. Tauris.

Rodrik, D. 2003. "Introduction: What Do We Learn from Country Narratives?" In *In Search of Prosperity*, 1–20. Princeton, N.J.: Princeton University Press

Rose, Pete. 1991. "Morality Politics and U.S. Refugee Policy." In *Rethinking Today's Minorities*, ed. Vincent N. Parrillo, 177–79. Westport, Conn.: Greenwood Press.

Rubenberg, C. 1983. *The Palestinian Liberation Organization: Its Institutional Infrastructure.* Belmont, Mass.: Institute of Arab Studies.

Rubin, Barry. 1994. *The PLO Under Arafat.* New Haven, Conn.: Yale University Press.

Rubin, Herbert, and Irene Rubin. 1995. *Qualitative Interviewing: The Art of Hearing Data.* Thousand Oaks, Calif.: Sage Publications.

Said, Edward. 1994. *The Politics of Dispossession.* New York: Pantheon Books.

Salam, Nawaf A. 1994. "Between Repatriation and Resettlement: Palestinian Refugees in Lebanon." *Journal of Palestine Studies* 24 (Autumn): 18–27.

Sayigh, Rosemary. 1978. "The Struggle for Survival: The Economic Conditions of Palestinian Camp Residents in Lebanon." *Journal of Palestine Studies* 7 (Winter): 101–19.

——. 1995. "Palestinians in Lebanon: Harsh Present, Uncertain Future." *Journal of Palestine Studies* 25 (Autumn): 37–53.

Sayigh, Yazid. 1997. *Armed Struggle and the Search for State.* Oxford: Clarendon Press.

Schiff, Benjamin. 1995. *Refugees Unto the Third Generation.* Syracuse, N.Y.: Syracuse University Press.

Scott, James C. 2009. *The Art of Not Being Governed: An Anarchist History of Upland Southeast Asia.* New Haven, Conn.: Yale University Press.

Seabright, Paul. 1993. "Managing Local Commons: Theoretical Issues in Incentive Design." *Journal of Economic Populations* 7 (Fall): 113–34.

Sekhon, Jasjeet S., and Rocío Titiunik. 2012. "When Natural Experiments Are Neither Natural nor Experiments." *American Political Science Review* 106 (February): 35–57.

Shapiro, Ian, and Stephen Skowronek and Daniel Galvin. 2007. *Rethinking Political Institutions.* New York: New York University Press.

Shaul, Mishal. 1986. *The PLO Under Arafat.* New Haven, Conn.: Yale University Press.

Shiblak, Abbas. 1997. "Palestinians in Lebanon and the PLO." *Journal of Refugee Studies* 10 (3): 261–74.

Shlaim, Avi. 1995. "The Debate About 1948." *International Journal of Middle East Studies* 27 (3): 287–302.

——. 2008. *Lion of Jordan.* New York: Knopf.

Shleifer, Andrei. 1997. "Agenda from Russian Reforms." *Economics of Transition.* 5(1): 227–31.

——. 2001. *Without a Map.* Cambridge, Mass.: MIT Press.

Sirhan, Bassem. 1975. "Palestinian Refugee Camp Life in Lebanon." *Journal of Palestine Studies* 4 (Winter): 91–107.

Smith, Charles. 2010. "World War II and the Creation of the State of Israel." In *Palestine and the Arab-Israeli Conflict: A History with Documents*, 165–221. New York: St. Martin's Press.

Soliman, Ahmed M. 2004. *A Possible Way Out: Formalizing Housing Informality in Egyptian Cities.* New York: University Press of America.

Steinmo, Sven. 2001. "The New Institutionalism." In *The Encyclopedia of Democratic Thought*, ed. Paul Barry Clark and Joe Foweraker. London: Routledge. http://stripe.colorado.edu/~steinmo/foweracker.pdf.

Sugden, Robert. 1989. "Spontaneous Order." *Journal of Economic Perspectives* 3 (Autumn): 85–97.

Suleiman, Jaber. 1999. "The Current Political, Organizational, and Security Situation in the Palestinian Refugee Camps of Lebanon." *Journal of Palestine Studies* 29 (Autumn): 66–80.

Takkenberg, Lex. 1998. *The Status of Palestinian Refugees in International Law.* Oxford: Clarendon Press.

Thelen, Kathleen. 1999. "Historical Institutionalism in Comparative Politics." *Annual Review of Political Science* 2 (June): 369–404.

——. 2004. *How Institutions Evolve.* Cambridge, Mass.: Cambridge University Press.

Tsai, K. S. 2002. *Back-Alley Banking: Private Entrepreneurs in China.* Ithaca, N.Y.: Cornell University Press.

Turki, Fawaz. 1972. *The Disinherited: Journal of a Palestinian Exile.* New York: Monthly Review Press.

Umbeck, J. 1981. *A Theory of Property Rights with Application to the California Gold Rush.* Ames, Iowa: Iowa University Press.

UNRWA. www.unrwa.org

UNRWA Report. December 2009. "Relief and Early Recovery Appeal (RERA) for Nahr al Bared Palestine Refugees, September 2008–December 2009." http://www.unrwa.org/sites/default/files/201007133727.pdf.

UNRWA Report. October 2010. "Reconstruction of Nahr el Bared Camp and UNRWA Compound. Progress Report 1: September 2007–October, 31, 2010." http://www.unrwa.org/sites/default/files/2011042974549.pdf.

UNRWA Report. December 2010. Relief and Recovery Support for Displaced Palestine Refugees from Nahr el- Bared Camp: Final Report: January to December 2010." http://www.unrwa.org/sites/default/files/2011072163951.pdf.

UNRWA Report. Spring 2014. "Voices from Yarmouk." http://www.unrwa.org/crisis-in-yarmouk.

Weimer, David L. 1997. *The Political Economy of Property Rights.* Cambridge, Mass.: Cambridge University Press.

Werker, Eric. 2007. "Refugee Camp Economies." *Journal of Refugee Studies* 20 (3): 461–80.

White, Ben. 2005. "Dispossession, Soil, and Identity in Palestinian and Native American Literature." *Palestine—Israel Journal* 12 (2&3): 149.

Yandle, Tracy, Nadya Hajj, and Rafal Raciborski. 2011. "The Goldilocks Solution: Exploring the Relationship Between Trust and Participation in Resource Management Within the New Zealand Commercial Rock Lobster Fishery." *Policy Studies Journal* 39 (4): 631–58.

INDEX